Marketing Cultural & Heritage Tourism

A World of Opportunity

By Rosemary Rice McCormick

*President, Shop America Alliance and
Co-Founder, U.S. Cultural & Heritage Tourism Marketing Council*

Routledge
Taylor & Francis Group

LONDON AND NEW YORK

Publisher's Note

The Museum Store Association previously published some content included in "Marketing Cultural & Heritage Tourism" in a series of cultural and heritage tourism white papers and articles for *Museum Store* magazine and *The Cultural Traveler* guide from 2007 to 2011, written by Rosemary McCormick and Sheila Armstrong. All content has been updated and reformatted for this book.

The Cultural & Heritage Traveler Study was conducted by Mandala Research in 2009 on behalf of the U.S. Cultural & Heritage Tourism Marketing Council, Shop America Alliance, Museum Store Association, Heritage Travel (a division of the National Trust for Historic Preservation)/ Gozaic and other sponsors in partnership with the U.S. Department of Commerce/Office of Travel & Tourism Industries.

About the Author

Rosemary Rice McCormick

Rosemary Rice McCormick serves as president of the Shop America Alliance, the travel trade association she co-founded in 1998, representing hundreds of the nation's premier shopping tourism destinations and museum stores. She is the publisher and editor of *Shop America* magazine, oversees development and marketing of Shop America Tours, and co-produces the annual ONE Travel Conference. Rosemary co-produced the landmark U.S. Cultural & Heritage Tourism Summit in Washington, D.C., in 1995. She is a founder of the U.S. Cultural & Heritage Tourism Marketing Council and co-publisher of *The Cultural Traveler* guide. Since 1993, Rosemary has directed McCormick Marketing, a strategic consulting firm specializing in global retail development, sponsorship and tourism marketing. Rosemary served as director of marketing for Mall of America, the nation's largest enclosed retail and entertainment center, from its groundbreaking through its grand opening, where she was responsible for marketing, tourism, public relations, sponsorship and events. She served as an official delegate at the historic White House Conference on Travel & Tourism and currently serves on the U.S. Travel Association board of directors/executive committee and the Destination & Travel Foundation board of directors. Rosemary lives in the Saint Louis area with her husband and children. She serves as a volunteer docent at the Saint Louis Zoo where she is involved in conservation education. She earned her bachelor's degree in marketing management from Mundelein College/Loyola in Chicago.

Marketing Cultural & Heritage Tourism
A World of Opportunity

Table of Contents

Photo Credits

Foreword

by Beverly Barsook
Executive Director, Museum Store Association

Shopping, dining and cultural travel are top tourism activities. In 2007, the Museum Store Association entered into a strategic partnership with the Shop America Alliance and the U. S. Cultural & Heritage Tourism Marketing Council to act as a catalyst for an emerging shopping and tourism niche called cultural heritage tourism. Retail stores in cultural venues offer a unique shopping experience and there are many opportunities for partnerships between shopping centers and cultural attractions.

Our project required educating our cultural venues about tourism and its potential to draw visitors and shoppers. As part of our partnership, we produced a series of white papers directed primarily at cultural attractions about the tourism industry. Little did we know that this new niche would be so popular! Many shopping centers, convention and visitor bureaus and destination marketers were also interested in how they could partner with their local cultural venues to present their cities' many assets. The Museum Store Association is delighted to be the publisher of an expanded, revised and updated fundamental manual on marketing cultural and heritage tourism.

You will find help with all of the following: the basics of cultural and heritage tourism, new insightful statistics about the cultural traveler, how to sell cultural tourism, partnership strategies, determining who your visitors are and how to market to them, marketing to cultural heritage tourists through merchandising, special events and PR, turning your team into tourism ambassadors, understanding the drive-market travel segment and promoting to groups. There are case studies of successful niche museum stores, dining and culinary tours, attractions, effective promotion via online and social media, and developing a cultural heritage tourism marketing plan.

"Marketing Cultural & Heritage Tourism" is an ideal publication for anyone looking for straightforward, practical information and examples of how to work with cultural venues, market your cultural assets and start partnerships. We could not have found a more enthusiastic and tireless supporter of cultural tourism and the potential of partnerships than our author, Rosemary McCormick.

Introduction and Welcome

I've always been passionate about tourism. My first real job at 16 was in concessions at the Saint Louis Zoo, one of the world's top-rated zoos, where I currently serve as a volunteer and meet guests from around the world. Later as a college student, I waitressed at baseball icon's Stan Musial's popular restaurant Musial & Biggie's, where Stan the Man's fans from near and far regularly packed the place. One of my career milestones was at Mall of America in Minnesota, where I served as the director of marketing from the groundbreaking through the grand opening of the nation's largest retail and entertainment center, attracting 40 million visits per year in a state with just over 4 million residents. I am grateful for these opportunities that shaped my perspectives on tourism's unique ability 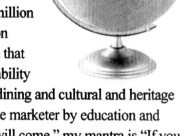 to deliver exceptional business for shopping, dining and cultural and heritage destinations. In addition, I am also a passionate marketer by education and avocation. So instead of "If you build it they will come," my mantra is "If you market it effectively, they will come—and spend!"

This book was written to address a significant opportunity to embrace marketing and tourism as a means to sustain and celebrate cultural and heritage treasures. I was inspired and encouraged to write "Marketing Cultural & Heritage Tourism" through our partnership with the Museum Store Association. Brainstorming and sharing ideas over the past several years with MSA's Executive Director, Beverly Barsook, and her MSA board, team and members, as well as with my colleague Sheila Armstrong with the U.S. Cultural & Heritage Tourism Marketing Council, we identified a need for elevating the importance of tourism as a business builder for cultural and heritage destinations. Toward that end we published a series of seven MSA white papers on tourism topics, launched our annual *The Cultural Traveler* guide for consumers and the travel trade, co-sponsored The Cultural & Heritage Traveler Study, and presented at many conferences including the ONE Travel Conference for Shopping, Dining & Cultural Tourism that we produce each January. This book is another step in sharing the wealth of success stories and opportunities that cultural and heritage tourism provides.

Cultural and heritage experiences are the heart and soul of travel and tourism. By exploring and sharing each region's unique cultural and heritage treasures, we all become better global citizens. Cultural and heritage tourism experiences are diverse, broad-based and touch almost every traveler in special ways.

"Marketing Cultural & Heritage Tourism" is a business development tool that you can use in several ways. It will define opportunities in cultural and heritage travel, and help you better understand the behavior of the cultural traveler and the importance of cultural and heritage experiences as part of leisure travel. You will learn ways to more effectively market cultural and heritage destinations to both domestic and international travelers with the goal of building attendance at, increasing incremental revenue for and ensuring the long-term viability of cultural and heritage attractions of all sizes. You will benefit from the experiences of others through case studies and interviews with experts, and you will be provided with strategic planning tools and guidelines for developing your own tourism marketing plan.

"Marketing Cultural & Heritage Tourism" is written for cultural, heritage and tourism marketing professionals, as well as directors, board members and communications professionals in cultural and heritage organizations. Museum store managers, buyers and other store personnel will find a wealth of information, as will educators and travel and tourism students. In addition, the book has valuable insights for community leaders and national, state and local tourism authorities. Tour operators, travel partners, travel writers and other media professionals also can gain useful information.

"Marketing Cultural & Heritage Tourism" is based on experiences and insights gathered from cultural and heritage leaders and locations throughout the United States, along with data from U.S. domestic leisure traveler studies and the U.S. Department of Commerce/Office of Travel & Tourism Industries. However, cultural and heritage travel experiences are also a global phenomenon. The recommendations provided in this book are relevant to cultural and heritage organizations and attractions worldwide. Your feedback and case studies are most welcome and may be featured in future editions of this book, in newsletters or online at USCHT.com. E-mail Rosemary McCormick at ShopAmericaTours@aol.com.

Chapter 1:

Tourism 101—The Cultural & Heritage Business Opportunity

You have probably opened this book because you are interested in growing visitation numbers and spending at your cultural or heritage attraction, museum stores and restaurants through increased tourism. Or perhaps you work in the tourism industry and are seeking improved ways to partner with your local cultural and heritage organizations. Or you are a student in a hospitality and tourism program, eager to learn more about the exciting world of cultural and heritage tourism. Or perhaps you are a media professional or other "culture vulture" interested in the latest trends. Whatever your depth of experience or perspective, "Marketing Cultural & Heritage Tourism" is dedicated to opening a new world of opportunities for you and your colleagues.

> "Travel is fatal to prejudice, bigotry and narrow-mindedness."
> —*Mark Twain*

In the time it takes for you to read this book and develop your cultural and heritage tourism marketing plan, millions of travelers will visit thousands of cultural and heritage institutions worldwide, and in doing so will gain a better understanding of our world and humankind. The goal of this book is to provide ideas and opportunities to help you enhance your market share within this growing sector.

What Is Tourism?

On Career Day at Chesterfield Elementary, my parent-volunteer role was to share my exciting career with my daughter's fourth grade class. I love my work in tourism marketing, but candidly it pales somewhat compared with the police officer who addressed the class right before me and answered questions like "what does it feel like to get shot?" He was a hard act to follow, especially with the 10-year-old boys.

To warm up the group, I asked them to describe what they think tourism is. The answers ranged from "it's when someone shows you around a place" to "it's when you get to stay in a hotel" to one kid who sadly confused tourism with terrorism and said "it's when bad guys fly planes into our tall buildings."

In fact, defining tourism can be a challenge for anyone. Let's start by describing tourism in general, and then define a branch of tourism referred to as cultural and heritage tourism. From there, we can begin to explore ways to effectively market cultural and heritage tourism to travelers.

The U.S. travel and tourism industry is defined as all travel, both business and leisure, domestic and international, short hop and day trips with travel of 100 miles or more, to and within the United States. Tourism is an amalgamation of several key industries including airlines, hotels, rental cars, railways, cruise ships, amusement parks, attractions, museums, golf courses, spas, retailers, restaurants, credit card companies, communities and more. Cultural and heritage organizations, attractions and destinations are a key part of the travel and tourism industry.

Travel and Tourism: A Major U.S. Industry*

- U.S. travel and tourism industry is one of America's largest industries
- $759 billion in direct travel expenditures, including domestic and international travelers
- $1.8 trillion in direct, indirect and induced tourism-related output, including international travelers' spending in the United States

Drives Commerce

- $118 billion in tax revenue for local, state and federal governments generated by direct travel expenditures
- Each U.S. household would pay $1,000 more in taxes annually without the tax revenue generated by the travel and tourism industry
- Direct spending by resident and international travelers in the United States averages $2 billion per day; $86.6 million per hour; $1.4 million per minute; and $24,000 per second
- 7.4 million direct travel-generated jobs; $188 billion travel-generated payroll
- 1 of every 9 U.S. non-farm jobs is created directly or indirectly, or is induced, by travel and tourism

One of the Largest Service Exports

- $134 billion spent by international visitors in the United States
- $103 billion spent outside the United States by U.S. residents
- $32 billion is balance of travel trade surplus for the United States

*Source: U.S. Department of Commerce/Office of Travel & Tourism Industries compiled by U.S. Travel Association, U.S. Travel Answer Sheet 2011, www.ustravel.org

The U.S. travel and tourism industry is defined as all travel, both business and leisure, domestic and international, short hop and day trips with travel of 100 miles or more, to and within the United States. Tourism is an amalgamation of several key industries including airlines, hotels, rental cars, railways, cruise ships, amusement parks, attractions, museums, golf courses, spas, retailers, restaurants, credit card companies, communities and more. Cultural and heritage organizations, attractions and destinations are a key part of the travel and tourism industry.

What Is Cultural and Heritage Tourism?

Cultural and heritage tourism is a branch of tourism that includes experiencing the performing arts, museums of all kinds, science and nature centers, zoos, aquariums, historic homes and sites, religious sites, artists and artisans, state/national parks and monuments, heritage trails and byways, and the special character of a place. It is often a blend of education, entertainment and preservation. And, it is experiential, meaning it seeks to involve and engage the visitor.

Cultural and heritage tourism is also a leading U.S. tourism sector in terms of dollars—**a $192 billion industry**, according to the 2009 The Cultural & Heritage Traveler Study. In fact, cultural and heritage tourism ranks

number three, behind only shopping and dining as the top travel activities in the United States, according to the U.S. Department of Commerce/ Office of Travel & Tourism Industries. Cultural and heritage tourism is among the fastest growing segments of the tourism industry. In addition, cultural and heritage travelers stay longer and spend more money than other types of travelers.

Cultural and heritage tourism does not normally feature sports, spas, casinos or theme parks. These are all important tourism activities and, as you may suspect, there are many exceptions to the rule of what is cultural and heritage tourism. Some museums, such as the renowned National Baseball Hall of Fame in Cooperstown, N.Y., and the World Golf Hall of Fame in Saint Augustine, Fla., are devoted to sports, but are nevertheless considered part of cultural and heritage tourism. Some theme parks celebrate cinematic pop cultural trends and others create a pop culture all their own. Theme parks like SeaWorld embrace natural and sustainable tourism, while some shopping centers feature touring exhibits, artwork, and even aquariums. Understandably, it is often a challenge to draw the line on what is considered cultural and heritage tourism. Or, as Garrison Keillor said at the 1995 White House Conference on Travel and Tourism, "All tourism is cultural tourism."

Marketing Cultural and Heritage Tourism: A New Trend

Cultural and heritage tourism is not new, either. In fact, it's one of the oldest, most revered and most universal forms of tourism worldwide. What is newer—and hence the topic of this book—is marketing cultural and heritage tourism. In recent years the cultural and heritage aspects of a place have been rediscovered as an important marketing tool to attract travelers.

Cultural and heritage institutions do not always focus on marketing, however, especially to tourists. Even in those institutions with enough resources to maintain a marketing/communications program, the primary outreach is to members, donors and the local community. Tourists, defined as visitors traveling 100 miles or more, who visit these institutions might be viewed as incidental "frosting on the cake" and don't always rank high in audience development or the marketing mix. In fact, strategic marketing to bring in more tourism visitors historically has been a rare occurrence, and limited research has been done to track tourism visitors. This has resulted in a lack of appreciation for the impressive spending habits of the cultural traveler.

Historically, the model of choice for funding cultural and heritage institutions has been public funding via tax support, private funding from donors/members and grants that may be a combination of private and public funding. When these sources become challenged, whether due to competition or economic factors, cultural and heritage institutions suffer, visitation and revenues decline, and the institution's core mission of sharing its collections and attractions and educating the public is compromised.

Marketing to attract more high-spending tourists is a viable way to monetize cultural and heritage institutions today. In fact, tourism marketing can be accomplished with minimal impact on the budgets of most cultural and heritage institutions and generate impressive return on investment, by using the strategies and tactics outlined in this book.

Chapter 1: Action Steps

1. Cultural and heritage tourism provides many unique opportunities for market differentiation and specialization for niche markets. Review and assess the cultural and heritage assets of your organization, district, town, city or region to develop experiential themes that will appeal to visitors.

2. Define tourism as a business-building opportunity within your cultural or heritage organization.

3. Evaluate cost-efficient ways to position and market your cultural and heritage assets to attract travelers.

Chapter 2:
The Cultural & Heritage Traveler Study

The groundbreaking research of The Cultural & Heritage Traveler Study, conducted in 2009, revealed that more than three-quarters of all U.S. leisure travelers participate in cultural or heritage activities while traveling, translating to 118.3 million adults each year. With cultural and heritage travelers spending an average of $994 per trip, they contribute more than $192 billion annually to the U.S. economy.

> "One's destination is never a place, but a new way of seeing things.
>
> —*Henry Miller*

"We discovered that an impressive number of U.S. travelers seek out cultural and heritage experiences," says Helen Marano, director of the Office of Travel & Tourism Industries, U.S. Department of Commerce. "With 78 percent of all domestic leisure travelers

participating in cultural and heritage activities, their expenditures confirm that this is a strong market, and they are contributing significantly to our communities."

Mandala Research conducted The Cultural & Heritage Traveler Study in 2009 for the U.S. Cultural & Heritage Tourism (USCHT) Marketing Council, in conjunction with the U.S. Department of Commerce/Office of Travel & Tourism Industries. Heritage Travel Inc., a subsidiary of The National Trust for Historic Preservation, and its website, www.gozaic.com, were lead sponsors of the study. Other sponsors included the American Association of Museums; California Travel and Tourism Commission; Center for Socioeconomic Research and Education at Texas A&M University; Chicago Office of Tourism; Positively Cleveland; Visit Florida; Condé Nast; *The History Channel Magazine*; Marriott International; the Museum Store Association; Sarasota and Her Islands Convention and Visitors Bureau; Shop America Alliance; Vantage Technology Partners; and the Virginia Tourism Corporation.

The study shed light on what travelers consider when making destination and spending choices—information you can use in your marketing strategies. It was also the first study to segment cultural and heritage travelers, showing the diverse groups that exist within this broader category. The segmentation analysis uncovered five types of cultural and heritage travelers: Passionate, Well-Rounded, Aspirational, Self-Guided and Keeping it Light. Three segments—Passionate, Well-Rounded and Self-Guided— were more serious about their travels and said that cultural and heritage activities had a greater impact on their destination choice. Together, these three segments represent 40 percent of all leisure travelers and contribute nearly $124 billion to the U.S. economy. (See more information about these segments later in the chapter.)

Cultural and heritage travelers as a whole are more frequent travelers, reporting an average of 5.01 leisure trips in the past 12 months versus non-cultural and heritage travelers with 3.98 trips. They also are more frequent business travelers and are more likely to have taken an international trip in the past 12 months than their non-cultural and heritage counterparts. More than half of travelers agree that they prefer their leisure travel to be educational, and nearly half report spending more money on cultural and heritage activities. They also are likely to travel further to get the experiences they seek; about half of most recent overnight leisure trips were 500 miles or more from home. More than a third say they traveled between 100 and 300 miles for a day trip.

The study found that cultural and heritage travelers are more likely to participate in culinary activities, such as sampling artisan food and wines, attending food and wine festivals, visiting farmers' markets, shopping for gourmet foods and enjoying unique dining experiences.

Other cultural and heritage activities identified by travelers include: visiting historic sites (66 percent); attending historical re-enactments (64 percent); visiting art museums/galleries (54 percent); attending an art/craft fair or festival (45 percent); attending a professional dance performance (44 percent); visiting state/national parks (41 percent); shopping in museum stores (32 percent); and exploring urban neighborhoods (30 percent). The vast majority of these travelers (65 percent) say that they seek travel experiences where the "destination, its buildings and surroundings have retained their historic character."

Top 10 Activities Considered Cultural & Heritage*

Activity	Percent
Attending cultural and/or heritage fair or festival	68%
Visiting heritage buildings/historical buildings	67%
Visiting historic sites	66%
Visiting Native American sites	64%
Attending historical re-enactments	64%
Visiting history museums/centers	61%
Visiting living history museums	60%
Participating in an organized tour of local history or culture	59%
Visiting natural history museums/centers	59%
Visiting art museums/galleries	54%

*Source: The Cultural & Heritage Traveler Study, 2009.

"This study of the habits of cultural and heritage travelers reconfirms the size of this lucrative market," says Scott Gerloff, president and CEO of Heritage Travel, the study's lead sponsor. "It also shows that cultural and heritage travelers seek authentic destinations with historic character as well as educational experiences in their travels."

Laura Mandala, managing director of Mandala Research, explains the methodology: "The study surveyed a nationally representative sampling of leisure travelers who identified themselves as cultural and heritage travelers. We first asked travelers if they had heard of the term 'cultural or heritage traveler,' then asked them to define what they thought the term meant. Later in the study we provided them with a definition of a cultural and heritage traveler and asked how well that statement described them. Based on their answers to these questions and the behaviors and attitudes they reported, we identified a range of types of cultural and heritage travelers. The study can benefit both the travel industry and cultural and heritage institutions because it identifies who these travelers are and how they think of themselves, which in turn can guide marketing and communications efforts to reach them."

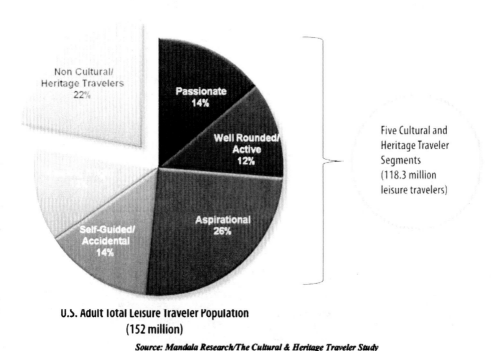

U.S. Adult Total Leisure Traveler Population
(152 million)

Source: Mandala Research/The Cultural & Heritage Traveler Study

The Cultural & Heritage Traveler Study: 15 Significant Findings

1. Seventy-eight percent of all leisure travelers, or 118.3 million U.S. adults, are cultural and heritage travelers.
2. Thirty-six percent of survey respondents have heard the term "cultural and heritage traveler."
3. Cultural and heritage travelers spent an average of $994 on their most recent leisure trip versus $611 spent by non-cultural and heritage travelers.
4. In 2009, cultural and heritage travelers had an estimated economic impact in the United States of $192.3 billion.
5. Although they demographically skew slightly older, cultural and heritage travelers are found in all age groups; they also are more educated and have higher household incomes.
6. Cultural and heritage travelers report an average of 5.01 trips in the past 12 months versus 3.98 of non-cultural and heritage travelers.
7. Cultural and heritage travelers are more frequent business travelers and are more likely to have taken an international trip in the past 12 months.
8. Cultural and heritage travelers are more interested in experiences where the destination, its buildings and surroundings have retained their historical character.
9. Explorers of different cultures, cultural and heritage travelers desire to learn about history and stimulate their minds; they like to be intellectually challenged by leisure travel.
10. More than half (58 percent) of cultural and heritage travelers want an educational experience when traveling for leisure.
11. Cultural and heritage travelers are more likely to participate in a wide range of leisure travel activities, visiting museums and historical sites, participating in culinary activities, attending food and wine festivals, visiting farmers' markets, and enjoying unique dining experiences as well as fine dining.
12. Nearly half (45 percent) of cultural and heritage travelers strongly/somewhat agree that they spend more money on cultural and heritage activities on a leisure trip.
13. More than one-third (37 percent) of cultural and heritage travelers will pay more for lodging that reflects the culture and heritage of the destination they are visiting.
14. An estimated 24 percent of all leisure travelers will take a cultural and heritage trip in the next 12 months. This equates to 36 million U.S. leisure travelers.
15. Cultural and heritage travelers are dedicated shoppers at museum stores (32 percent). They also shop outlets, galleries, unique/authentic retail and traditional retailers and brands.

Five Defining Traveler Segments

As mentioned earlier, the study segmented travelers into five groups based on the level of influence cultural and heritage activities played in their travel decisions. From a marketing perspective, rather than simply lumping all cultural and heritage travelers together, it is strategic to note the variables in the five segments and use this information in planning your messaging. For example, a Civil War battle site or museum would primarily target travelers with Passionate interest in this era of American history, while botanical gardens may attract visitors in Passionate and Aspirational segments.

The five segments are defined as follows.

1. Passionate: These travelers seek out cultural and heritage trip activities because they have a strong desire to participate in such activities when they travel.

- Segment includes 14 percent of leisure travelers or 21.4 million.
- Represents all demographic groups but statistically more likely to be male, belong to the Silent/GI generation, hold a graduate/professional degree and have a household income of $100k+.
- Cultural and heritage activities are a key driver in their destination choice.
- They travel more often and are more likely to take long weekends (three to four days) rather than longer cultural and heritage trips.
- When planning a leisure trip, they are most likely to use the websites of the destination (77 percent).

2. Well-Rounded/Active: These cultural and heritage travelers are open to experiencing all types of activities while on a leisure trip.

- Segment includes 12 percent of leisure travelers or 18.4 million.
- Represents all demographic groups but statistically more likely to be male, belong to Generation X, hold a graduate/professional degree and have a household income of $100k+.
- Cultural and heritage activities are a key driver in their destination choice, although they are open to experiencing all types of activities while on a leisure trip.

- Eighty-one percent strongly/somewhat agree that they seek travel experiences where the destination, its buildings and surroundings have retained their historic character.
- When planning a leisure trip, they are most likely to use general Internet searches (54 percent) and friends and family members (51 percent). In addition, they are more likely to look for packaged deals.
- Like the Passionate and Aspirational segments, they are more likely to pay more for lodging that reflects the culture/heritage of the destination.

Travel Across the Generations
The generations referred to in this book are described as follows:
Generation Y (Gen Y): Born 1984–2002
Generation X (Gen X): Born 1965–1983
Baby Boomers: Born 1946–1964
Silent/GI Generation: Born 1927–1945

3. Aspirational: They desire to participate in cultural or heritage activities, but had limited experiences during their most recent trip and during the past three years.

- Segment includes 25 percent of leisure travelers or 38.2 million.
- Represents all demographic groups but statistically more likely to be female, belong to the Baby Boomer generation and hold a high school/ GED degree.
- They desire to participate in cultural and heritage activities but have not done so on their most recent leisure trip or on a leisure trip in the past three years.
- Eighty-four percent strongly/somewhat agree that they like to bring back local/ regional memorabilia from the places they visit, sharing them with their friends and family.

- Ninety-eight percent think it's very/somewhat important to choose activities on their leisure trips that are relaxing and relieve stress.

- Along with Passionate and Well-Rounded travelers, they are more likely to say they will pay more for lodging that reflects the local culture and surroundings.

4. Self-Guided/Accidental: Travelers in this segment take advantage of cultural and heritage activities while on a leisure trip, but cultural and heritage activities are not the driver for their destination choices. They most often prefer exploring small towns, galleries and self-guided historical tours.

- Segment includes 14 percent of leisure travelers or 21.4 million.
- Represent all demographic groups but statistically more likely to be male, belong to Gen X and the Silent/GI generation, and live in the West/Midwest census regions.
- They prefer taking advantage of cultural and heritage activities in which they can guide themselves (museums, exploring small towns, historical sites, etc.).
- Seventy-six percent strongly/somewhat agree that they seek travel experiences where the destination, its buildings and surroundings have retained their historic character.
- Ninety-four percent think it's very/somewhat important to choose activities on their leisure trips that create lasting memories.
- They are more likely to take a week-long cultural and heritage trip, rather than shorter trips, and they are more likely to start their trip planning without a specific date or destination in mind.

5. Keeping it Light: Travelers in this segment don't seek out cultural and heritage activities, but will attend what they perceive as fun art, cultural and musical events.

- Segment includes 12 percent of leisure travelers or 18.4 million.
- Represents all demographic groups but statistically more likely to be female, belong to the Boomer generation and live in the Midwest census regions.
- Cultural and heritage activities are not a driver of their destination choice. Rather, they take advantage of the activities that are available once they arrive at a destination.

- Their cultural and heritage trips are more likely to be weekend getaways rather than longer trips.
- They prefer taking advantage of cultural and heritage activities in which they can guide themselves (museums, exploring small towns, historical sites, etc.).
- Eighty-six percent strongly/somewhat agree that they prefer taking trips that are a combination of a wide variety of activities, such as culture, shopping, nature, exercise and dining.
- Ninety-two percent think it's very/somewhat important to choose activities that enrich their relationship with their spouse, partner and/or children.

Chapter 2: Action Steps

1. The cultural and heritage traveler is a large, affluent market. To market to these travelers more effectively, study the five market segments to gain a greater understanding of behaviors and preferences.

2. Target these frequent cultural and heritage travelers to build repeat visits.

3. Feature educational experiences in your tourism messaging, because 58 percent of cultural and heritage travelers view these as important.

Chapter 3:
Marketing and Monetizing Cultural & Heritage Tourism

The more you, as a cultural or heritage tourism professional, embrace the importance of attracting tourists to your institution and serving their needs, the more successful and economically viable your organization will be. As obvious as this may seem to some, cultural and heritage organizations must more fully adopt the marketing strategies that will lead to directly achieving funding goals. This is especially critical during tough economic times when traditional sources of funding for cultural and heritage organizations are challenged.

> "Travel is more than the seeing of sights; it is a change that goes on, deep and permanent, in the ideas of living."
>
> —*Miriam Beard*

The Funding Challenge

Cultural and heritage institutions are frequently funded by a combination of sources including:

- Donor/member contributions
- Grants
- Admission fees
- Special events
- Local tax funding
- Sales from the institution's stores and restaurants
- Other revenue from traveling exhibits, etc.

With the exception of local tax funding, travelers and tourists can enhance income in all of these areas. For example, repeat tourists are excellent membership prospects if you offer an "out of town" special membership package that caters to the occasional visitor. These guests are the perfect targets for your special events. Special travel grants and sponsorship programs can be used to fund cultural organizations. Travelers eat out three times each day so your restaurant or café can benefit from their appetites. And retail sales from the institution's stores have the opportunity to benefit most from the traveler, because shopping is a top tourism activity.

Marketing Your Organization to Tourists

Marketing is the process used to determine what products or services may be of interest to your customers, and the resulting strategy to use in sales, communications and business development. Cultural and heritage organizations and attractions will benefit from a strategic marketing plan that has one or more elements of the plan focused on attracting tourists as museum visitors.

While tourists are different from local visitors, marketing strategies for both segments are closely aligned. For example, many tourists stay with friends and family (called VFR in tourism talk—Visiting Friends and Relatives) and go where they are taken or directed by their hosts. When the museum, zoo or aquarium is noted as the "best of" in the area, locals take their VFR guests there to share a sense of pride. Tourists who stay in hotels are also strongly influenced by "local favorite" recommendations gleaned from the Internet, guidebooks, restaurant and hotel staff, as well as total strangers.

Tourism is a relationship-driven business. To strengthen your relationship with the diverse tourism audience and market more effectively to them, start with information on these key points:

- Who is your tourism customer?
- How can you identify and track tourists?
- What motivates tourists to visit your cultural or heritage destination?
- What motivates tourists to shop, dine and spend money at your institution?

Who Are Your Tourism Customers and How Can You Track Them?

Once you understand that tourism is a key business segment that can drive incremental visits to your institution and sales at your store, your focus will naturally shift to attracting more tourists and tracking their spending.

It's important to note that not all tourists have the same propensity to spend. You can easily discern that if your museum collection and retail merchandise target model train buffs, for example, attracting the right demographic and psychographic profile will yield the greatest sales. Similarly, certain types of tourists spend more than others. International visitors typically outspend domestic travelers by up to 10 times. Baby Boomers typically outspend seniors or student groups. We can offer many broad generalizations here that, candidly, will not be as helpful as the information you can glean from your own tracking, observations and the tourism market research that should be available from your local convention and visitors bureau.

It is essential to have ongoing systems in place to track tourists and their spending. The results will be very positive—even surprisingly high in most cases—and will justify your efforts to increase tourism business.

You can track tourists in many ways, from license plate counts and simple guest books that ask for city/state/country to sophisticated point-of-sale (POS) systems that capture ZIP codes and visitor intercepts. Tracking doesn't have to be complex or overwhelming. Often a simple, friendly "where are you from" will elicit the tourism information that your staff can track.

Train your staff to start looking for tourists and recognize them as a special sub-set of your customer base that will spend more and have different needs and wants. Following are just a few ideas you may find helpful to incorporate into your tracking system.

Five Effective Ways to Track Tourists

1. **Special exhibitions.** These events often attract out-of-town guests and provide a perfect opportunity to track sales. Be sure to encourage visitors to sign your guest register book or sign up for your mailing list. Make sure you capture customer ZIP codes or country of origin. With this system you can do follow-up marketing, determine the impact of exhibition sales on your tourism business and monitor your overall tourism during normal periods versus special event periods.
2. **Parking lot license surveys.** Your museum may want to track tourists with parking lot license surveys on an ongoing basis. While not 100 percent statistically accurate due to rental cars or tourists coming with friends and families, in many markets this provides a quick and easy snapshot of when you have a higher percentage of out-of-state visitors.
3. **Track cost-efficient, pre-arrival marketing.** Partner with your local convention and visitors bureau (CVB) and other attractions to distribute information out of your market prior to the traveler ever leaving home. Known as pre-arrival awareness, this strategy is very influential and measurable if you include an incentive offer for a free gift with purchase or a minimal discount at your attraction or store. Track responses and share your results with your team as you build and refine your distribution.
4. **Tracking key items helps you sell more.** Use tracking to determine your store's best sellers for tourists. Often these will be unique items with local flavor. Share this information with your tourism partners

for public relations purposes. If the items are affordable, offer special rates for bulk orders of these unique items for tradeshow gifts or provide to hotels as freebies in the rooms.

5. **Build a relationship with your local convention and visitors bureau (CVB) sales team.** They are responsible not just for marketing the area and its hotels, but also bringing guests to your venue and store. One idea: Offer to host a special event, such as an in-store wine and cheese reception for travel agents, travel media and tour operators who bring business into your market. The CVB is always looking for unique venues and yours may be perfect. If your organization is a member of the CVB (highly recommended), make sure all key staff members are copied on leads, newsletters and sales reports. The CVB tracks the business they bring to the community and can assist you with ideas and opportunities, at little or no cost. Chapter 4 will provide more strategies for forming win/win partnerships with your CVB and others to help promote tourism at your cultural destination.

What Motivates Tourists to Shop?

Why do most travelers shop? It's fun! Plus they find great deals and discover

wonderful treasures. Travelers enjoy extending their positive experiences when returning home by showing or wearing prized purchases and sharing their personal travel stories. Shopping, dining and cultural experiences are consistently ranked as the top three travel activities in the United States, contributing jobs and economic benefit to millions while enriching travel experiences overall. Most tourists are motivated to shop by a combination of the following factors:

Seven Reasons Tourists Shop

1. **Unique**—Tourists are looking for merchandise that can't be found back home, evokes a sense of place, is part of a special event or

experience, or is simply something they do not have easy access to elsewhere, i.e., artwork, jewelry or books on a favorite topic to name a few examples.

2. **Value/price**—A better deal than back home is a very strong motivator for international visitors, especially when exchange rates are in their favor.

3. **Time to shop**—Visitors on vacation will buy items they can find back home, simply because they are in a more relaxed, stress-free vacation mode with time to indulge in recreational shopping.

4. **Planned expenditure**—Many tourists budget for souvenirs or allow for extra money to treat themselves while on vacation.

5. **Shop with family and friends**—A shopping entourage provides encouragement to buy, i.e., "That looks good on you!"

6. **Extend the experience**—Tourists like to shop for mementos from the destination or event.

7. **Obligation**—Traveling offers a unique opportunity to find a gift or souvenir for a loved one left behind, or as a thank you for the baby sitter, pet sitter or house sitter.

Just as important as understanding the primary motivation to shop is understanding barriers to buying.

Seven Reasons Tourists Do Not Buy

1. **Can't take it with them**—Travelers have concerns about transporting their purchases or having to deal with extra luggage or difficult shipping issues. *Solution:* Make shipping easy and display prominent signage that states, "We ship anywhere."

2. **It's not unique or special**—Visitors don't want to shop for things they can find elsewhere, like another cheap key ring. *Solution:* Merchandise with a clear point of view and share the unique stories of your products via your sales staff or visual merchandising.

3. **Assortment issues**—Sales will be lost if the visitor can't find the right size, style, quantity or color desired. *Solution:* Make it clear that you can do special orders and ship anywhere.

4. **Stress**—When shopping with family or friends at the end of their visit, others in the party may be tired or eager to leave. *Solution:* Provide options for purchasing after they leave your institution, such as through a catalog or online store. Consider adding comfortable seating with magazines or a play area to entertain the non-shoppers while the primary shoppers browse.

5. **Access**—If visitors don't see your store, they don't know it's there or what treasures you carry. Requiring paid admission to shop in the store is another deterrent. *Solution:* If the store's location is difficult to find, provide signage or merchandise displays at the point of admission and make sure visitors can gain access to the store without an admission fee.

6. **Poor customer service**—Inattentive sales staff and long lines at the register will cause visitors to leave your store without making a purchase. *Solution:* Continually train your staff on key customer service principles and reward them for excellent service.

7. **Weak visual merchandising**—Uninteresting displays and poor lighting will not entice customers into your store, let alone help them make a purchase. *Solution:* Tell a story with your merchandise displays.

With this background in mind, let's look at how to use partnerships in building more tourism business—the topic of the next chapter.

Chapter 3: Action Steps

1. Establish and monitor systems to track tourism visits to your venue and spending in your store.

2. Review the "Seven Reasons Tourists Do Not Buy" and determine if any of these are impacting your sales. Implement action steps for improvement.

3. Leverage your local marketing and communications efforts to support your tourism marketing because many tourists are visiting friends and relatives.

Chapter 4:
Partnership Strategies to Build Tourism Business

Remember the fable "Stone Soup"? This is a classic tale of partnership strategy and innovation. The story goes that a hungry traveler arrives in a remote village with no money and no food can be found. We're talking zero, zip, nada. The sad-faced villagers insist that they are all poverty stricken and facing starvation. The clever traveler commiserates with the villagers and then suggests that he will prepare his delicious and nutritious stone soup, a secret recipe which he promises will feed the entire village if only someone could provide a large pot and a few logs for a fire. The villagers are skeptical, but one woman has an oversized caldron that she agrees to loan.

> "Perhaps travel cannot prevent bigotry, but by demonstrating that all peoples cry, laugh, eat, worry, and die, it can introduce the idea that if we try and understand each other, we may even become friends."
>
> —*Maya Angelou*

The traveler fills the pot with water from the village well, sets it on a wood fire pit in the center of town and throws in a carefully selected large stone. The villagers gather to watch as he stirs and tastes the stone soup and proclaims: "This delicious stone soup is just missing a few key ingredients. It would be so much better if we only had an onion and perhaps a little salt." At which point one villager remembers he has a few onions saved from the last harvest and another has some salt. These are quickly added to the stone soup.

A few minutes later, the traveler again tastes the soup and notes it just needs a few carrots and perhaps some garlic or a pinch of pepper. A few hungry villagers then run home and reappear with carrots, pepper and garlic. After more stirring and tasting the traveler enthuses on how tasty the soup is now, but how much better it would be with a just few more veggies, some beans, potatoes or whatever, and would anyone happen to have a few small scraps of meat, perhaps. By now, the villagers have all gathered to watch the spectacle of the bubbling caldron. Smelling the garlic and onions, they are enthralled. Several dash home and manage to find other key ingredients and bring them back to toss in the pot, and so on and so on, tasting and adding this or that, until finally the traveler declares the stone soup has reached perfection and is ready to serve. By this time the villagers have set up tables around the stone soup pot, found some bread, wine, fruit and cheese to share and someone is playing music. It has become a party! When the stone soup is served, there is plenty for all, and the traveler is lauded as a hero.

The Power of Partnership

This story illustrates the power of partnership and the synergy that can be developed in your tourism marketing strategy. We start with the basic premise that no one has enough budget, time or resources to do tourism marketing on their own, just as none of the villagers had enough food to make a complete meal. To be successful in tourism, it really "takes a village" to market the destination as a whole, along with your venue or store, as a "must visit" component of the location. With this approach, you can easily identify your core group of potential partners—your "villagers"—who will share your tourism goals and help you leverage your own marketing resources.

The most logical first step is to develop a win/win partnership between your cultural and heritage institution and local tourism authorities, such as the convention and visitors bureau (CVB) or destination marketing organizations (DMOs), including state tourism offices, conference and visitors associations, chambers of commerce, and so on.

While there are some stellar examples of success that we will share later, most cultural and heritage organizations miss these key opportunities. DMOs throughout the country regularly comment and, yes, even are heard to complain that "cultural people do not 'get' tourism."

By the same token, some DMOs do not "get" cultural and heritage attractions or related retail activities. They understand how important it is to market their community's cultural and heritage treasures, and they have the best of intentions. However, DMOs have many masters to serve and respond to trackable programs designed to put "heads in beds," which serve their lodging partners and ultimately generate the essential taxes that fund most DMOs.

There are ways to turn this reality to your advantage, however. Consider this: Hotels face a major business challenge every day, or in their case, every night, and that is driving occupancy, which historically averages around 60 percent or less nationally. Hotels need ways to fill up these unsold rooms almost every night. Packaging and partnering with cultural and heritage attractions can help. Clearly, then, there is an opportunity to strengthen partnerships between DMOs, their hotel constituents and cultural and heritage institutions and contribute to the success of all involved.

Think of CVBs and DMOs as your tourism partners. They have knowledge, research, resources and ideas that can help you to refine your own tourism strategy.

How to Prepare Your Partnership Plan
STEP 1: Create your own organization/attraction partnership profile.
Start with an outline of what you can bring to the table to support tourism marketing. It may include the following elements:

1. Your venue—Offer the use of your facilities for tourism events or meetings (either free or at an attractive fee).

2. Your image—Your position in the community as a cultural or heritage leader is a prestigious affiliation for other tourism entities.

3. Your location—Highlight your proximity to other tourism attractions and lodging, or, if you are off the beaten path, indicate that it's worth the extra effort to visit.

4. Your budget—List any funds or in-kind marketing you are prepared to invest in tourism marketing. In-kind marketing can be links from your website to the CVB site, or discounted tickets to your next special exhibit to package with hotel stays.

5. Your research tracking—Share data on where visitors are coming from, domestically and internationally, if your store or your institution tracks visitors (highly recommended). These reports are valuable to your partners.

6. Your incentives and gifts—Produce special regional, themed or logo merchandise you can provide for your tourism partners to distribute. You can sell these items at a discounted rate or donate items.

7. Existing tourism relationships—List your memberships in the CVB or chamber of commerce, the hotels or transportation partners you currently work with, tour operators or online travel partners, etc.

8. Website—Create a travel information page where your partners can be listed on your website with reciprocal links to their sites.

9. Special promotion opportunities—Allow tourism partners to place approved brochures or other marketing tools in your institution at a designated information desk or other appropriate area.

10. Creativity and ideas—Your museum special events and limited-time exhibitions are great tourism opportunities that your partners can help to promote, building their business and yours.

11. Airport venue—Some museum stores, for example, have airport retail outlets that provide a great opportunity to communicate with tourists.

12. Docents and volunteers—You can tap into this excellent source of free labor for special events or ongoing tourism projects, including parking lot license surveys.

13. Resources for design and production—Using your own agency or freelancer to produce cooperative marketing materials paid for by other partners provides an added value at limited cost, plus gives you more control over the final message and image.

14. Packaging components—Offer a discount on purchases or a gift with purchase at your venue's store for inclusion with other partner packages.

15. Giveaway components—Donate a shopping spree (e.g., $100 gift certificate) at your store to tie into a contest to win a trip to your destination, in exchange for the promotional consideration and media value of the event.

16. Your institution's tourism opportunities—If you know you already attract quite a few German travelers who come to see your unique German artists collection, or families from the surrounding states who come during the fall and winter weekends, use this information to connect with other partners targeting the same audiences. For example, airline partners who target German travelers will want to promote your museum and its special collection of German artists. Hotels with low weekend occupancy will create packages highlighting your attraction for family weekend getaways. When you know who your target is, you can become the hook in your partners' marketing campaigns.

STEP 2: Identify your potential tourism partners.

The key question to answer here is "got tourists?" (Note that we define tourists as both business and leisure travelers, international and domestic, including anyone residing more than 100 miles from your location.) The following organizations or businesses could potentially make good tourism partners. List each potential partner that fits with your marketing goals and create a database with key contact information.

1. Your Marketing and Communications Team

Your number one tourism marketing asset is your own internal marketing and communications team. You need to be fully aware of your organization's strategy on tourism and how you can work in tandem to market a visit to the site, including shopping in your store and dining in the café or restaurant, if you have those options, as valuable parts of the overall experience. Sit down and talk with your marketing/communications colleagues. Share with them the value of tourism spending in your market, your organization partnership profile and your interest in developing more productive tourism partnerships to share your institution's mission with a broader audience and generate more visitation.

2. Local Convention (or Conference) and Visitors Bureau (CVB) or Destination Marketing Organization (DMO)

Most CVBs and DMOs require membership. It's a wise investment that your institution probably has made already. But don't just be a member; maximize your membership. Show up for meetings and events. Speak up and advocate for the importance of cultural and heritage tourism. Volunteer to be a part of key initiatives and sign up for events and promotional partnerships.

By maximizing your membership, you will build your tourism knowledge, develop networks and increase your access to important tourism information, research and partners. Become an active member and ask to serve on committees and sit on the board, if possible. Be willing to host events, participate in FAMs (familiarization tours for tour operators and travel agents or media) and donate items for fundraisers. In short, be a true partner.

As Mike Gallagher, CEO of CityPASS and a California Travel & Tourism Commission board member notes, "To be an effective member of the tourism community, the one word you need to know is YES!" (Read more about CityPASS in Chapter 11.)

3. State Office of Tourism

View your state office of tourism as an extension of your marketing team. Most have all the information you need to get started marketing, along with current research online. They also may offer cost-efficient opportunities for you to join them in co-op sales missions and travel tradeshows. A little research here will be highly productive and educational.

Depending on where you are located, your state office of tourism may provide free marketing and public relations support or have a "pay-to-play" membership/partnership arrangement similar to CVBs. Increasingly, state and local tourism offices are very interested in showcasing cultural and heritage tourism because it elevates the tourism business from "heads in beds" (hotel occupancy) to a strategy that highlights the unique qualities of the destination for tourists and local residents alike.

Many state tourism directors are appointed by the governor, so the person in this position may change with the outcome of elections. And even though the staff usually remains, new directors often mean that the overall tourism philosophy and approach change. Tourism is at times a very political business, so it's wise to stay on top of local and national political trends and to lobby your representatives to support pro-tourism initiatives.

Also keep in mind that the state office of tourism is funded by your tax dollars, so you should be highly proactive in asking for their partnership in promoting your institution or organization. Again, the key word is "partnership," meaning that in order to get you must be prepared to give. Attend your state tourism conference. Know your state tourism director and key executives. Ask for a copy of their annual plan and budget, and find out about grant and co-op marketing opportunities. When appropriate, contact your state's representatives who work internationally and educate them about your cultural and heritage offerings.

4. Regional Tourism Organizations

You will become aware of these via your CVB and state tourism affiliations and as you broaden your tourism network. Regional tourism organizations exist in most parts of the country and are essentially independent marketing cooperatives and/or lobbying organizations for regional tourism initiatives. Examples include the Southeast Tourism Society (www.southeasttourism.org), California Travel Industry Association (www.caltia.org) and the Texas Travel Industry Association (www.ttia.org), to name a few. Some offer tourism packaging and itineraries online that can feature your cultural and heritage organization or a special offer from your venue and store.

5. National Tourism Organizations

Check out partnership opportunities with the following national organizations:

- **U.S. Department of Commerce (USDOC)/Office of Travel & Tourism Industries (OTTI)** is an example of our government at work for you with travel research, information and statistics. USDOC tracks international tourists to the United States and advises the Secretary of Commerce on tourism policy with the help of a 30-person appointed Travel & Tourism Advisory Board. Some research is available online free of charge. Custom research studies can be very helpful. (www.tinet.ita.doc.gov)
- **U.S. Travel Association** produces International Pow Wow, the largest international travel tradeshow in the United States. They also

are an excellent resource for travel and tourism contacts, research and information. You must be a member to access their services, but membership is a wise investment if you plan to market to international travelers and want to be a voice in the travel industry. (www.ustravel.org)

- **Corporation for Travel Promotion (CTP)** is a public/private partnership with the mission of promoting increased international travel to the United States. Formed in 2010 to market the United States globally, it administers a projected annual $200 million marketing fund created by the Travel Promotion Act. CTP is governed by an 11-person board of directors appointed by the Secretary of Commerce. No membership is required; co-op marketing opportunities are in development. (www.corporationfortravelpromotion.com)

- **National Tour Association (NTA)** is the leading association for professionals serving travelers to, from and within North America. Since its founding in 1951, the association has served a broad and diverse membership and helped them expand market reach with innovative business tools, strategic relationships and collaboration within the industry. NTA membership represents more than 40 countries. (www.NTAonline.com)

6. Niche Tourism Organizations

These organizations focus on a select business niche (e.g., motorcoach travel, student travel, auto travel, group tours, culinary tourism, shopping tourism, cultural tourism) and can be very large, like AAA/CAA with more than 51 million members, or very select. When you affiliate and partner with any of these organizations, have a clear objective in mind so you develop the right relationships and maximize your return on investment. Some examples include:

- In addition to roadside service, AAA/CAA offers consumers many travel planning services, such as help booking air, hotels and car rentals, and finding cruises. Their Show Your Card & Save program helps drive retail sales and track tourists. Read more about partnering opportunities with AAA in Chapter 8. (www.aaa.com)

- **International Culinary Tourism Association** was organized to help people, communities and businesses thrive by forging mutually beneficial relationships based on a universal interest in food and drink. They offer cuisine and cultural partnerships and educational outreach. (www.culinarytourism.org)
- **Shop America Alliance** is the travel trade organization representing hundreds of the premier shopping tourism destinations, retailers, shopping centers, museum stores and outlets in North America. Founded in 1998, Shop America Alliance co-produces the annual ONE Travel Conference, SASI-ONE Awards and *The Cultural Traveler* guide, publishes *Shop America Magazine* and markets more than 200 shopping tours in 40 cities. (www.shopamericatours.com)
- **U.S. Cultural & Heritage Tourism Marketing Council (USCHT)** is a travel trade association with a mission to market U.S. cultural and heritage tourism experiences. USCHT represents leading U.S. tourism destinations, attractions and travel partners engaged in marketing U.S. culture and heritage to travelers throughout the United States and around the world. USCHT co-produces the annual ONE Travel Conference, SASI-ONE Awards and *The Cultural Traveler* guide, and sponsors market research on the cultural and heritage traveler. (www.USCHT.com and www.TheCulturalTraveler.com)

Other important tourism organizations and websites are listed in Appendix A of this book.

7. Hotels and Lodging Partners

When partnering with hotels, your best contact initially is the sales director, as he or she knows when they need to push their inventory at non-peak times and are often very creative. The hotel's marketing and communications professionals also may be involved. There are several types of hotel partnerships that work well including:

- **Concierge and front desk programs**—Educate, train and/or provide incentives for concierges or hotel front desk staff to send visitors to your institution or store. This works very well when you have a special exhibit or event. This may sound basic, but for these teams, periodic personal visits with a supply of your brochures and a special treat for the group (e.g., cupcakes, cookies, candy—food seems to do the trick best) can work wonders. Consider tying your outreach to special holidays or times of year so that you get noticed; for example, "Our Museum Loves Our Hotel Partners" for Valentine's Day; "Summer Surprises from Our Museum to Our Hotel Partners"; or "Thanks a Million from Our Museum" at Thanksgiving.

- **Packaging programs**—Package discounted admission to your cultural institution or a special store offer with other tourism elements, i.e., added-value discounts as part of a hotel's accommodation package. The hotel partner will do the promoting and marketing, at little or no cost to you, other than possibly providing your institution's logo and photo.

8. Local/Regional or Themed Cultural and Heritage Tourism Partners

Visitors at cultural institutions will often visit multiple cultural and heritage attractions in the same area, so even while you are competing for their time, these venues also are your natural partners. Destinations that establish and promote their arts and cultural focus through cooperative marketing are able to promote and bring more business to all. Think of arts districts and cultural progressive events, or areas like Forest Park in Saint Louis where the world renowned zoo, art museum, history center and other fine museums and family attractions create critical mass for locals and tourists.

9. Tour Operator Partnerships

Tour operators are often seen as the "holy grail" of tourism marketing. Tour operators are essentially wholesalers who package and resell tours, tickets and accommodations to various markets including domestic group tours (students, senior groups, etc.), international group tours, foreign or frequent independent travelers (FIT), travel agents and online travel agents.

To partner with tour operators, you must be included in their tariff (schedule of prices) or catalog of offerings, and offer a net rate, which is a discounted admission, so that they can make a profit selling your experience. Museums with paid admissions and museum stores, for example, can play in this arena if they offer a special discount that tour operators will then promote as added value. We will explore tour operator partnerships in greater depth in a Chapter 8.

10. Transportation Providers

Planes, trains, motorcoaches and automobiles are all essential means of travel, so it makes sense to explore these partnership opportunities. Airlines are frequently involved as sponsors and marketing partners for cultural events and can tie in to "getaway giveaways" that can feature your cultural and heritage institution. If your collection has special appeal to one key travel segment, e.g., Chinese or German travelers, your public relations department should pitch the in-flight magazines that reach this audience and also feature any related merchandise and special exhibits that you offer.

Gray Line Tours developed a very creative Spy Tour of Washington, D.C., working with the International Spy Museum. The two-hour tour featured more than 25 of Washington's most notable espionage sites and gives tour participants—"recruits in Spy School 101"—an opportunity to participate in an interactive mission as well as hear tales of the spies who left their invisible mark on the city. Recruits were briefed by a "training officer" on key sites linked to intelligence triumphs, disasters and mysteries. High-level former intelligence officers provided video briefings and trade secrets as the tour winds its way through the city. Each participant of the tour received a pop-up map of spy sites of the city—an item that is sold in the museum's gift shop.

11. Shopping Centers, Outlets and Retail Partners

Traditional shopping centers, outlet centers and department stores offer great potential for cultural and heritage partners. Since shopping and cultural

tourism are closely aligned, offering both in one package is appealing. For example, tourism consultant Pat Lee with the Cherry Creek Shopping District in Denver, Colo., developed a unique marketing partnership with several hotels. Lee explains: "We work with the JW Marriott, Four Points by Sheraton, Holiday Inn, Loews Denver and Hampton Inn and Suites. When guests stay overnight at one of the participating hotels, or bring a friend or family member living more than 50 miles away from Denver to Cherry Creek Shopping Center, they receive a 'Passport to Shopping,' with discounts to stores and restaurants, plus one free admission to one of Denver's cultural attractions, including the Denver Art Museum, Denver Botanic Gardens, Denver Zoo or Red Rocks Park and Amphitheatre. It's a win/win for the entire community."

12. Travel Media

Travel trade and consumer media tend to be fairly open with regard to their advertising/editorial mix. Be prepared to ask for extra editorial coverage or negotiate other added value when you place an ad in most travel media. You may be well advised to run a small ad to ensure good editorial placement.

On a larger scale, the travel media can provide excellent promotional partnerships—promoting, for example, contests to win a museum store gift certificate as part of a city getaway sweepstakes. In addition, international travel trade media representatives are often knowledgeable resources about their target audiences. Developing good working relationships on all levels with key publications will prove beneficial to your advertising, PR and promotional goals.

13. Museums on Us

Museums on Us is another great partnership example. I first learned about it from my local Bank of America ATM machine. Now that's innovative marketing! On the first full weekend of every month, Bank of America and Merrill Lynch cardholders have the opportunity to visit—at no charge—more than 150 popular cultural landmarks taking part in Museums on Us. Designed to provide a benefit to Bank of America customers and increase access to the arts across the United States, Museums on Us is in its 14th season.

The program brings new audiences and attention to participating organizations, which range from some of the nation's most celebrated museums and regional gems, including art, science and history museums, as well as zoos and aquariums. The Metropolitan Museum of Art, Chabot Space & Science Center, Motown Museum and National Cowboy & Western Heritage Museum all participate in the Museums on Us program.

To qualify for Museums on Us, customers simply present their Bank of America or Merrill Lynch credit or debit card along with a photo ID to gain free general admission to any participating institution on the first full weekend of each month.

STEP 3: Develop your tourism partnerships.

Armed with your cultural heritage organization partnership profile, which we recommend you print on your letterhead as a Tourism Opportunities Overview, and a list of your potential tourism partners and key contact data, you are prepared to enter the partnership development arena.

The most important element of this step is developing solid win/win relationships. As mentioned earlier, tourism is a highly relationship driven business. It is more effective to invest time developing and cultivating the right relationships than any type of financial investment in media or marketing programs. If you are fortunate to have colleagues within your institution who have already established tourism relationships, team up and leverage these. This can be as simple as hosting the annual CVB member reception and offering a special gift or store discount to all attendees. Or plan to attend the CVB and state tourism meetings with your institution's senior staff. Be visible, be involved and be willing to say YES!

If you find a void in tourism relationships within your organization, start now to build them by reaching out strategically to those in your potential tourism partners' database. The best way to do this is to call and invite your potential partner to coffee or lunch, preferably at your institution, so they can be immersed in your world. Give them your VIP Tour. Share your partnership profile, your target audiences and brainstorm how you can best work together. Your potential partner will be impressed with the list of opportunities you are willing to bring to the table and likely will offer similar opportunities from their organization or business.

It's important to focus on the bottom line in these meetings, which means "what's in it for me" from your potential partner's point of view. For example, the CVB will see an opportunity to enhance its membership and/ or community approval rating by more aggressive promotion of cultural and heritage tourism with your institution showcased. The hotel will see more opportunities for weekend bookings with the special package featuring family getaways and your institution. Other cultural partners will see co-op opportunities in presenting all the great things to do and see at your destination as part of a compelling package.

The goal of all these discussions is to expand your ability to attract visitors and ring the register at your institution, so make sure your store has the opportunity to capture visitors by including an offer or gift with purchase that brings guests into the store. For hotel packages, you can even include a gift item that the hotel agrees to reimburse. The key is to make sure guests pick up their gift in store, not at the hotel. What's in it for you? You'll benefit from more visitors to your cultural institution, increased retail traffic, incremental business you can track and positive PR.

Partnership Discussion Topics

When you meet with your tourism partners, plan to discuss the following:

1. How is business? Your goal is for your potential partners to openly share their tourism business goals and opportunities with you. You both want more tourism business. How can you work together to achieve this?
2. Position your institution and your store as tourism destinations. Share any data you have and any observations on the target markets you attract.
3. Your openness to working with the right partners. Share your interest in building long-term win/win relationships.
4. Your list of tourism opportunities. How do these sync with your potential partner's strategy and objectives? Discuss the partner's top opportunities.
5. Others who may partner with you. Ask for referrals and build a network.
6. Next steps. Create a timeline and follow-up points. If you are new at this and/or lack back-up resources, start small and build. Your primary objective is forging strong relationships so you can easily reach out in the future and create ongoing opportunities.

Strategic Partnership Plan—Documentation and Review

Once you agree to enter into a marketing partnership, clearly document who is doing what and when. Send this information to all parties involved in a written document. Depending on your internal protocol, this could be a

signed letter of agreement or simply an e-mail outlining your mutual understanding, use of logos and images, and so on.

Include goals that are quantifiable, e.g., number of room nights booked, number of guests presenting their hotel partner voucher at the institution's store for their free gifts or media value of the article in the in-flight magazine. Whatever you plan to do, document it in the agreed-upon format and include reasonable expectations and measures of success so you can evaluate the partnership in terms of how it drives

business. Also include a time for post-evaluation review of the partnership to determine if goals were met or exceeded and what can be done next time to improve the promotion. This step leads to the long-term relationships that are so important in your overall strategy.

Choose Wisely

Choose your partners wisely so they will enhance your organization's image and positioning. Make sure all parties will benefit from the partnership and any disputes can be quickly and easily resolved.

One of our colleagues insists that all his agreements carry a "flip of the coin" clause, which means that disputes, if they arise, will be resolved in this very straight-forward manner. While we do not recommend this approach in all cases, the point is that you should only enter into partnerships where the relationship is strong and there is a shared win/win ethic.

Tourism Partnership Strategies Drive Cultural Travel: A Case Study

By Sheila Armstrong, Executive Director, U.S. Cultural & Heritage Tourism Marketing Council

Your budget has been cut, traffic has diminished, sales are down and even the morale of your staff is suffering. Like all businesses in this economy, cultural and heritage organizations and their stores are challenged just to stay even with last year's figures. Such challenges require creative, innovative selections.

Keep in mind that we're all in this together and by reaching out to find like-minded partners, you can get support not only for your morale but, more importantly, you can partner together to develop marketing strategies that will drive visitors to your destinations.

How do you start? First, evaluate what you have to offer potential partners. A good way to do this is by identifying all of your assets that that not only benefit you but also could benefit your partners. For example, your location, your venue and your position in the community could be leveraged for partnership value.

Next, look for inspiration from partnership examples. Chicago is a great place to begin searching for that inspiration. The city has dedicated significant tourism resources to marketing itself as a destination for cultural products and experiences. It has a long-standing reputation for innovation in positioning Chicago as an appealing visitor destination that informs, inspires and entertains with the focus on its cultural and heritage offerings.

Chicago has an Office of Tourism and Culture and a Department of Cultural Affairs and Special Events. It also has the Chicago Park District. These are remarkable resources, and, no doubt, more than most communities have. But each of these offices and the many cultural entities in the city can nevertheless provide a myriad of ideas on how to partner to maximize resources.

Karen Vaughan, former director of communications for the Chicago Office of Tourism, shared some insights on how this all works. That office serves as the marketing company for the city, highlighting destinations and promoting seasonal initiatives. Many destinations can be inspired by looking

at how this great city pools resources and partnerships to drive visitor traffic.

For example, cultural institutions often have the opportunity to capitalize on city-wide events to drive business to their destination at minimal or no cost to them. The Oriental Institute Museum – University of Chicago illustrates how seizing partnership opportunities delivers great value. Even though the institute has a minimal marketing budget, it has gained extensive exposure and increased visitation by partnering with the Chicago Department of Cultural Affairs and Special Events and the Chicago Office of Tourism and Culture on major events. The Oriental Institute often creates activities to complement the city's themed events. At other times, it reaps exposure by simply providing basic information about the institute and asking to be included in marketing communications. This is a great example of how expressing an interest and willingness to partner and support a larger outreach effort requires little investment and can result in high returns.

Chicago creates overarching marketing themes for the cultural community to capitalize on, but there are also organizations that identify a common goal and complementary resources to create their own cultural marketing initiatives. An example of this is the Art Institute of Chicago, which has a long-standing tradition of partnership with other organizations to develop tourism strategies that will engage different targeted groups of visitors. For example, the institute partnered with the Poetry Foundation, the Chicago Council – Global Affairs and the Chicago Symphony Orchestra on a year-long promotion called 360 Degree Globalization. This marketing initiative involved international consulates hosting receptions, musical performances featuring international destinations, poetry readings and themed art exhibits. Promotion for these events included a dedicated website devoted to all of the activities. The museum shop at the Art Institute capitalized on the theme by featuring global merchandise.

Eva Silverman, director of Arts and Community Engagement for the Chicago Office of Tourism and Culture, organizes a group called the Chicago Cultural Network. This organization comprises representatives of the arts and cultural communities. They meet regularly to update each other about their programs, connect and share concerns. Along with informal networking, Eva also invites speakers to share marketing information and education. The result is new partnerships formed and collaboration opportunities identified.

When looking for partners, keep an open mind on how you might create a new partnership initiative, even when at first glance, there doesn't appear to be a fit. For inspiration on this approach, look at the Adler Planetarium and Astronomy Museum and the National Museum of Mexican Art's marketing collaboration. The development director of the museum, Randy Adamsick, explains that the National Museum of Mexican Art started by identifying key parameters for working with partners, including looking for partners who were truly serious about collaboration and also serious about reaching out to the Hispanic community. The Adler Planetarium demonstrated these attributes, so the two organizations partnered on an ongoing program called

Under One Sky. The Adler also has added Spanish to all signage and offers free admission to the planetarium to all members of the National Museum of Mexican Art. The results are increased awareness and visitation at both facilities.

In addition, don't overlook foundations as a partnership resource. An example is the Terra Foundation for American Art, which is dedicated to providing funds to educational and cultural institutions for the purpose of promoting and educating the public about America's cultural richness. In 2008 the foundation funded a $3 million multi-year marketing program, American Art American City. All Chicago organizations that featured American art were invited to participate in the program. The vision was to implement a city-wide initiative to promote awareness and appreciation of historical American art, shining a spotlight on exciting collections, programs and exhibitions found throughout Chicago.

Cathy Domanico, director of tourism for Chicago Convention and Tourism, implemented yet another innovative way to work in partnership to drive visitors to Chicago and its cultural institutions. She organized sales missions to communities within the Chicago drive-market to tell them about the benefits of visiting Chicago. Whom has she invited to go with her to tell this story? Representatives of the cultural community.

Finally, an exciting marketing tool with partnership opportunities is Chicago's website, www.ExploreChicago.org, which serves as a resource and a platform for all Chicago has to offer its visitors. All cultural destinations are encouraged to have information on the website about their venues and special events. The website also speaks to these economic times by highlighting free events in Chicago to encourage visitors and residents alike to enjoy the city. Cultural destinations are invited to be included in this list as well.

Chicago is fortunate to have such a strong base for marketing its cultural and heritage assets, and to have extensive resources to support and generate tourism to its remarkable institutions and cultural experiences. Beginning with the mayor, city officials recognize the value of culture to both residents and visitors. They also recognize that nurturing the culture of collaboration generates a much more vibrant marketing platform to benefit all. So take a page from Chicago's partnership inspiration and begin today to nurture your own collaboration of partners to market your destination. Be an innovative, open-minded and inspiring leader in building partnership strategies to drive your tourism business. By working together, you can be much more successful than by working alone.

Chapter 4: Action Steps

1. Join and get fully involved with your local convention and visitors bureau or tourism organization. Be visible, be involved and be willing to say YES!

2. Create your own organization/attraction partnership profile to help identify your potential tourism partners.

3. Select the most appropriate partners based on your tourism goals and markets. Well-defined objectives, written agreements, tracking mechanisms and a review process should all be incorporated into your tourism marketing partnerships.

4. Develop your tourism partnerships. Effective partnerships are built on solid relationships with common goals and win/win strategies. Cultural and heritage organizations can develop effective partnerships with tourism professionals on local, regional, national and international levels.

Chapter 5:
Targeting Your Most Productive Visitor Prospects

Research from various resources, including The Cultural & Heritage Traveler Study discussed in Chapter 2 and the U.S. Department of Commerce/Office of Travel & Tourism Industries, indicates that travelers who shop and engage in cultural and heritage tourism are frequently big spenders. Plus, they stay longer and have a better overall experience. Motivated by these facts, seek out and attract these types of travelers for your cultural or heritage attraction and its related shopping opportunities.

Think International

The first step is to find out where cultural and heritage travelers come from— including international markets. International tourists, in fact, spend more than domestic tourists, so start by looking at your city's or region's propensity to attract international inbound travelers. The following charts show arrival trends from the top inbound markets for cultural and heritage travelers.

Overseas Cultural Heritage Visitors

[thousands of visitors]	2004	2005	2006	2007	2008	2009	2010	Change 2010/2004
Overseas Visitors	10,629	11,620	14,106	15,148	14,217	13,494	15,369	4,740
% Change	-	9	21	7	-6	-5	14	45
Share of Overseas Visitors	68.7	58.9	64.3	82.9	70.4	82.7	71.2	2.5
Point Change in Share	-	-14	9	29	-15	17	-14	

Source: U.S Department of Commerce/Office of Travel & Tourism Industries

U.S. Destinations Visited by Overseas Cultural Heritage Travelers

Visitation to U.S. Destinations/Regions (3)	Market Share 2010 (Percent)	Volume 2010 (000)
REGIONS		
Middle Atlantic	48.4	7,439
South Atlantic	30.1	4,626
Pacific	26.6	4,088
Mountain	16.8	2,582
New England	8.0	1,230
Pacific Islands	7.6	1,168
East North Central	7.0	1,076
West South Central	5.1	784
STATES		
New York	45.5	6,993
California	25.2	3,873
Florida	18.0	2,766
Nevada	13.6	2,090
Massachusetts	6.3	968
Hawaiian Islands	5.4	830
Illinois	5.0	768
Arizona	4.6	707
Pennsylvania	4.4	676
New Jersey	3.8	584
Texas	3.8	584
Georgia	3.1	476
Utah	2.8	430
CITIES		
New York City	44.8	6,885
Los Angeles	15.7	2,413
San Francisco	13.7	2,106
Las Vegas	13.3	2,044
Miami	10.1	1,552
Washington, D.C.	9.6	1,475
Orlando	8.4	1,291
Boston	5.9	907
Chicago	4.9	753
Honolulu	3.9	599
San Diego	3.7	569
Philadelphia	3.0	461
Atlanta	2.7	415
Phoenix	2.3	353

Source: U.S Department of Commerce/Office of Travel & Tourism Industries

Country of Origin of Cultural Heritage Visitors

Visitor Origin	Market Share 2010 (Percent)	Volume 2010 (000)
WORLD REGIONS		
Europe	55.5	8,530
Western Europe	53.2	8.176
Asia	19.2	2,951
South America	12.7	1,952
Oceania	6.1	938
Middle East	2.5	384
Eastern Europe	2.2	338
COUNTRIES OF RESIDENCE		
United Kingdom	16.7	2,567
Germany	8.9	1,368
Japan	7.5	1.153
France	7.0	1,076
Brazil	6.1	938
Australia	5.4	830
Italy	4.2	645
Korea, South	4.0	615
Spain	3.3	507
Netherlands	2.8	430
P. R. of China	2.7	415
India	**	**

Source: U.S Department of Commerce/Office of Travel & Tourism Industries

Main Purpose of Trip

Main Purpose of Trip (top 5 of 8)	2010 (Percent)
Leisure/Rec./Holidays	60
Visit Friends/Relatives	21
Business/Professional	11
Convention/Conference	4
Study/Teaching	4

Source: U.S Department of Commerce/Office of Travel & Tourism Industries

Information Sources Used by Cultural Heritage Travelers to Plan Trip

Information Sources Used (multiple response: top 4 of 12)	2010 (Percent)
Personal Computer	48
Travel Agency	36
Airlines Directly	24
Friends/Relatives	19

Source: U.S Department of Commerce/Office of Travel & Tourism Industries

Activity Participation While in the United States

Activity Participation While in the U.S. (multiple response--top 10 of 25)	2010 (Percent)
Shopping	90
Dining in Restaurants	86
Visit Historical Places	68
Sightseeing in Cities	59
Art Gallery/Museum	41
Cultural Heritage Sites	41
Visit Small Towns	37
Amusement/Theme Parks	34
Visit National Parks	34
Concert/Play/Musical	29

Source: U.S Department of Commerce/Office of Travel & Tourism Industries

In terms of international arrivals to the United States, the best is yet to come! The forecast from the U.S. Department of Commerce/Office of Travel and Tourism Industries is bullish:

- 51 percent overall inbound tourism growth between 2009 and 2015
- Similar growth across Canada, Mexico and overseas
- Led by China, Brazil, South Korea and India

Who's Coming to Your Area?

We've just been through a lot of data. So what's the bottom line? In thinking about your tourism plan, first be realistic, then strategic. Yes, it is great news that world tourism is growing by 4 percent annually and that U.S. international arrivals are projected to grow from 60 million in 2010 to nearly 83 million by 2015, with the average international traveler spending $3,600 per person per trip. Plus, there are another 118 million Americans who like to engage in cultural and heritage travel who are taking five or more trips per year. But what does this mean for you and your institution's visitation?

Start by analyzing who is coming to your area already. This information, as detailed in Chapter 4, is available from your state tourism office and local

CVB. Also factor in anything new that is planned, i.e., your airport has announced new direct flights from the London twice a week, or a major new development is planned in partnership with a Japanese firm that will send a large number of its management personnel to your area and so on.

Next, determine from among your key inbound markets who is the most likely to visit your cultural and heritage institution and how much they are likely to spend. Then look at logical opportunities to work with tourism partners in your area to increase your share of these key markets. You may consider something as simple as posting a welcome sign in other languages at a scenic point in your cultural or heritage institution, encouraging the sharing of photos via social media, and taking a picture of your smiling team members with the welcome sign and using the photo on your website, social media and other tourism marketing.

Who Is Spending Money?

Cultural and economic trends influence both visitation and spending. Japanese and Chinese guests, for example, are historically among the highest spenders per capita due to their tradition of gift-giving and buying in multiples. At the time of this writing, the Canadian and Australian dollars are on par with the U.S. dollar, creating a flurry of spending from these inbound markets. Likewise, the heightened value of some international currencies compared with the U.S. dollar means that the United States is on sale for international travelers, who find the quality and value of shopping in the United States superior to any other destination.

Consider how happy these international visitors are to spend their travel savings shopping in your store or visiting your institution. Everything is a terrific bargain from their point of view. In fact, Shop America Alliance's International Shopping Traveler studies in 2009 and 2010 show that international travelers spend on average more than $1,000 per person per trip on shopping!

The Travel Promotion Act: New Opportunities
for Cultural and Heritage Tourism
By Sheila Armstrong, Executive Director,
U.S. Cultural & Heritage Tourism Marketing Council

The following is an excerpt from a document prepared in 2011 as background for
a letter of recommendation from the U.S. Department of Commerce's Marketing
Outreach and Coordination Committee to the U.S. Secretary of Commerce's Travel &
Tourism Advisory Board.

The passage of the Travel Promotion Act in the spring of 2010 has presented an
unprecedented opportunity for everyone involved in the U.S. travel industry to create
a much more robust industry. In particular, those involved or interested in becoming
involved in marketing cultural and heritage tourism have an unparalleled opportunity to
be one of the greatest beneficiaries of the passage of this act.

The Travel Promotion Act of 2009 (H.R. 1299) calls for the establishment of The
Corporation for Travel Promotion as a nonprofit public/private partnership organized for
the purpose of promoting foreign leisure, business and scholarly travel to the United
States, and maximizing the economic and social benefits of that travel for communities
across the country. This mandate is to be accomplished through marketing and
other programs designed to position the United States as a destination of choice for
travelers. Learn more at www.corporationfortravelpromotion.org.

The act also created a funding method to support this marketing with an annual
budget not to exceed $200 million. Fifty percent of the program's funding will be
through a combination of cash and in-kind donations. Those funds will be matched by
international visitor payments of $14 per person collected by the recently established
Electronic System for Travel Authorization (ESTA).

The act specifically requires that the Corporation for Travel Promotion must benefit
all 50 states, including areas not traditionally visited by international travelers. This
has the potential to be particularly beneficial to the vast array of destinations and

businesses that cannot currently afford to market to international inbound travelers. For the first time, all destinations across the country will have the opportunity to benefit from platforms specifically designed to showcase attractions that are "off the beaten path." This opens up many possibilities for increasing the return on investment of marketing to the cultural and heritage traveler.

The Corporation for Travel Promotion advisory board is evaluating roles and responsibilities of the various organizations and has seen a need to identify how to best categorize and compellingly package the "product" that we are selling—the many experiences that our vast and diverse country has to offer the visitor. This is an opportunity for cultural and heritage tourism marketers to create new ways to provide these "products" in user-friendly, easily edited formats that allow travelers to search and/or book. Future planning should emphasize travel-themed options in appealing, compelling categories that inspire visitors' decision-making process and assist them in developing their travel plans.

One of the most effective ways of marketing our country is to tell America's story with thematic experiential travel itineraries and develop thematic tour products that are inclusive of natural, cultural and historic assets. These tours will attract a cross-section of audiences to multiple sites and events, and can transcend beyond geographic boundaries. By linking similar assets together as a linear "string of pearls," these types of travel options will motivate the visitor to travel and explore by interests—thus expanding opportunities for them to stay longer and spend more.

Travel and tourism to major cities, national parks and attractions in the United States are already a draw for international leisure and business travelers. There also are a number of smaller attractions, cities, villages, towns and communities that are beginning to offer cultural experiences that appeal to travelers seeking more intimate experiences. These destinations can stimulate domestic and international tourism, as well as provide jobs and increased commerce for local residents and businesses.

There also is a growing trend to develop thematic trails throughout the United States. There are music trails, wine and food trails, art and antique trails, historic trails devoted to African American freedom, the Civil War or women's issues, even a dinosaur trail. These trails will continue to proliferate and add value by telling the varied stories of our country.

However, there are some major issues that must be addressed to ensure the future growth of the cultural and heritage travel segment, as well as the travel industry overall. We must continue to push for better air travel, visa processing and welcoming doors throughout the country. We must look at options that will make travel more convenient, green and affordable, both for large cities and the many small towns and rural destinations that add color and enriching experiences to visitors. We should explore high-speed rail, fuel-efficient cars, buses, and even bicycles and Segways as optional means of transportation. Signage and electronic communication, such as mobile apps, also should be addressed to facilitate ease of travel and encourage visitors to expand their travel destination options.

We have the opportunity to improve how we tell the story of America, showcasing its breadth and depth of rich and colorful travel experiences, not only in our gateway cities and iconic destinations, but also beyond these key destinations, to add memorable experiences for visitors. In the future, we can and should do a better job of developing these experiences so visitors can thoroughly enjoy their travels and want to visit time and time again. We must help them learn more about our nation's unique natural, historic and cultural resources, as well as the creative talents that define our country's unique character, by weaving in the shopping, dining, and cultural and heritage experiences that are as diverse as our landscape.

Domestic and Drive-Market Travelers

Domestic travelers account for 90 percent of all travelers in the United States, and although they may spend less than international visitors, they are the top market for most cultural and heritage attractions. They also will spend significantly more than local shoppers—two to four times more in most cases. This is because of the "vacation factor"; they have planned to shop or purchase souvenirs as part of their travel experience. There are also those domestic travelers who are "power shoppers," or whose special interests attract them to your store's unique selections. By being aware of these patterns, you can merchandise and promote to help all visitors achieve their shopping goals and take home significant memories from your cultural and heritage institution.

In addition, as we'll explore in detail in Chapter 8, 85 percent of all travel in the United States is drive-market travel. Work with your CVB to identify the top domestic drive- or fly/drive-markets in your area and ways you can reach them most effectively. For example, the student group market is highly productive for some museums, historical attractions, zoos and aquariums. This market tends to be seasonal and relatively easy to target. Senior/Boomer group tours are another key market. If you plan to build this business, incorporate ease of access for motorcoaches into your marketing plan. By and large, however, the independent leisure market and/or family market are the top domestic markets for most cultural and heritage destinations.

As you develop your target market strategy, share your thinking with other key players in your organization. Together, visualize and strategize ways to use special events, promotions and PR to target and attract your most lucrative tourism market segments.

Chapter 5: Action Steps

1. Target your tourism marketing to those segments, e.g., international, domestic, families, students or seniors, that provide the best opportunities for your cultural and heritage organization.

2. Work with your CVB on international tourism marketing opportunities. They can share data on where visitors are coming from and how to grow this market.

3. Welcome the world! Create welcome signs in several languages for photo ops as part of your marketing outreach.

Chapter 6:
Merchandising, Special Events and Public Relations

Merchandising, special events and public relations initiatives all provide opportunities to get your attraction's message out in positive ways that can increase visitor numbers and dollars spent at your institution. This chapter takes a look at each.

The Merchandise Is the Message

Smart marketing starts in-store for tourists and locals alike. Your guests and shoppers have a unique opportunity to experience your organization's brand and message via your store's merchandising. In fact, in the cultural commerce world, the merchandise *is* the message. Books, DVDs, CDs, posters, special exhibit-related items, collectibles, logo items and home décor, as well as gifts and apparel that impart a sense of taste and style, all become an extension of your organization and share your story with current and future guests.

"Twenty years from now you will be more disappointed by the things you didn't do than by the ones you did do. So throw off the bowlines, sail away from the safe harbor. Catch the trade winds in your sails. Explore. Dream. Discover."

—*Mark Twain*

Merchandise is a very powerful form of sustained tourism marketing. Your home may include a favorite Georgia O'Keeffe print from the Georgia O'Keeffe Museum in Santa Fe, N.M., a poster from the National Gallery of Art in Washington, D.C., plus beautiful and unique autumn leaf-shaped placemats from the Adirondack Museum store in upstate New York. These all become valuable viral marketing for the museums' stores when shoppers share their finds with family and friends. The items spark conversation about travel experiences and ideas for future trips.

Special Events Build Tourism Business

Special events are essential to successful cultural and heritage tourism marketing. They provide consumers with excitement and a "must-see" sense of urgency. They can be particularly effective in attracting key tourism segments.

Here are three ways to use special events to increase your cultural and heritage tourism business:

1. **Major exhibits or special seasonal events** can be hosted and promoted by the institution and include merchandising in the store to support the special occasion. This is the most prevalent type of event and one that successful stores are experts at maximizing. It is critical to have a wealth of merchandise themed to relate to both your permanent collection and special exhibits, make plans well in advance and promote the merchandise with your organization's communications team.

2. **Special store events** can be independent of what is happening at the institution and are highly appealing to individual and group travelers. These are traditional retail events including:

    -   Seasonal sales
    -   Clearance sales
    -   Pre-holiday open houses
    -   New retail collection preview events
    -   Charity fundraiser shopping events
    -   Special events showcasing an artist, designer or author whose work you sell

    These retail events can cater to members only or target key groups, such as charities or other organizations interested in your collection.

3. **Customized events** that cater to your target markets are the greatest

opportunity for growth in the tourism arena. Consider implementing the following:

- Open early or late when bus tour groups are arriving and provide a private event.
- Schedule an artist or author event to coincide with a group tour visit.
- Theme your events to communicate your institution's unique features with costumed docents or special regional refreshments, as appropriate.
- Host a wine and cheese reception for your local tourism groups, inviting staff from your conference and visitors bureau (CVB), hotel concierges and tour operators. Give them a discount and gift during the reception. Ask them to refer their guests.
- When an international group, such as Japanese travelers, is coming to your institution, schedule a special event for them and offer to bring in interpreters from a local college. This is cost-efficient for you and a great way for language students to learn and network. Display a welcome sign in various languages; it's a visitor-friendly symbol that speaks volumes.
- Schedule private docent tours and events for groups of 20 or more, including a special discount, and offer this to tour operators and travel partners.
- Integrate special shopping events with your restaurant. For example, the very clever Baboon Brunch at the Brooklyn Zoo is a group tour opportunity with a boxed brunch and zookeeper chat, while guests watch the baboons eat. This event is fun, educational, income-generating and a retail sales opportunity for merchandising related to baboons and primates.

Public Relations and Media Communications for Tourism Development

Your special events are news. They give the media another reason to talk, write about and promote your cultural and heritage institution—and unlike advertising, media coverage is free. And they give your spokesperson a special tourism positioning opportunity, i.e., "we expect this event to draw guests from a 300-mile radius" or "we have groups coming from as far as China for this major exhibit."

As you plan your annual special events schedule, consider including the types of activities suggested above. Be creative in your event planning and collaborate with your organization's communications team so they can help you maximize your events for your ultimate goal—free media coverage and increased business.

Schedule a meeting with your organization's public relations professional and strategize ways to communicate your events to your target tourism audiences. Discuss the following:

- High-quality photos and succinct media releases.
- A feature on your website.
- Announcements on local and state tourism websites. They are eager for fresh content.
- Announcements to travel writers and the travel media. Access lists of travel media from resources including the Society of American Travel Writers, Shop America Alliance, the U.S. Cultural & Heritage Tourism Marketing Council and your local CVB, or work with TravMedia.com to distribute major event announcements worldwide.
- Announcements to local cultural and lifestyle/entertainment media.
- Announcements to regional and national travel, airline, fashion, lifestyle or home media. Depending on your event focus, the story and the visuals, you can generate a lot of great coverage from these media outlets.
- Announcements to tour operators, local hotels and concierges.
- Word of mouth from your members. Visiting friends and relatives (VFR) are one of the top forms of tourism.
- Announcements to local, regional, national and international organizations interested in your unique exhibit, collections or retail event.

- E-news and e-invitations to your own visitor database.

In addition, all media releases from your institution should include information on the store as a key part of the overall visitor experience. Talk to your organization's PR professional and make sure he or she is aware of the importance of the store.

As a publisher of an international magazine, *Shop America*, we solicit input and accept media information from various sources, we can share what works. Those that provide timely input with attractive, professional, high-resolution photos (300 dpi) and brief but complete copy have the best opportunity for inclusion. It is essential that you work with the communications professionals on your team and position your event message within the context of the total organization's message. This will greatly increase your chance of successful placement and will position your organization as a key contact for future media coverage.

Position Your Store as a Tourism Attraction

In all your media communications, consistently state that your attraction and your store are among the top destinations for visitors to your city or region. By repeating and reinforcing this message with anecdotes, photos of tour groups, research data (if available), international welcome signage in your store, a "we ship anywhere" policy, etc., you will build and enhance your tourism business. Don't underestimate the power of word-of-mouth marketing and the influence of visiting friends and relatives (VFR). Depending on your location, VFRs can account for 50 percent of all travelers and is especially strong with emerging markets such as India, Korea and China.

When travelers stay with local friends and family, the locals become tour guides. When exposed to your consistent tourism media messages, locals will think of you when deciding what to do and where to take their guests. They will recall that your institution is frequently noted as one of the most visited places in your city and will proudly take their guests there.

Make sure locals also hear your shopping message. For example, press releases might state, "Shopping is the most popular activity of all tourists in the United States. The most unique shopping spot in (your city) is at (your store) where visitors throughout the nation and around the world are always welcome."

Cherry Creek Shopping Center in Denver has used this strategy very effectively for years to position itself as one of Denver's top attractions. Macy's in New York City also uses this strategy. It works in any size market. The key is consistency.

Shop Talk—Retail PR Ideas

To optimize your organization's ability to get out a retail message to the media, it is often helpful to have what we call an internal "shop talk." Following are some ideas to get you and your colleagues thinking about generating more media coverage for your store:

1. Invite your local travel writers and radio and TV reporters to lunch and a tour of your store. Learn what topics they tend to feature and how best to feed them stories. Generally, e-mail is preferred, and high-quality (300 dpi) photos are welcome.
2. Develop a list of media that should receive your standard releases and keep it current.
3. Follow up your media releases with a call to confirm that they have received your e-mail and ask if they need any additional information or photos.
4. Include quotes in your releases.
5. Invite the media (or pitch an exclusive interview) to a particular event, such as an author who is visiting your store for a book signing.
6. Consider placing stories in your feeder market media. For example, if your customers are coming from Cincinnati to Detroit to visit your attraction, pitch a story in the Cincinnati city magazine and travel sections of the city newspaper to promote your theme/special show

and highlight your complementary merchandise.

7. Feature your merchandise on your museum's website. Keep it fresh by highlighting new merchandise and/or seasonal selections.

8. Work closely with your institution's communication/PR department to ensure that your message is on point.

As for store pitches (ideas that entice the media to use you in their stories), brainstorm creative and even unconventional ideas that call attention to your store:

- Provide story ideas tied to merchandise/gifts for special holidays. This can be tailored to children, special interests, collections, etc.
- Highlight merchandise that is exclusive to your store or merchandise that is uniquely produced in your area and provides a sense of place.

- Highlight merchandise that will be remembrances of the visitor's experience at your attraction, especially merchandise that has been designed and produced specifically for a special event or exhibition.
- Mention the "hot" items that fly off the shelves. Share these with the media for coverage around holidays or gift-giving seasons.

Look for ways you can get additional media coverage in local, regional and national travel and tourism publications. Ask your CVB's PR professional to help you target your stories to the travel and tourism media and include this individual on your media list. Check out opportunities to be part of travel media FAM tours (familiarization tours) as a way to get travel writers to include your store in their articles.

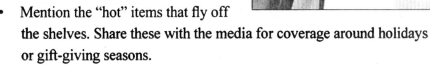

Tracking and Sharing Tourism Data

As discussed earlier, a key component of tourism marketing is collecting and analyzing data including: 1) where tourists are coming from, 2) where they are staying, 3) how much they are spending at your cultural and heritage institution and in your store and restaurant, and 4) what they are buying (trends to help your future merchandise planning). All this data has another use: If appropriate to release to the public, it could be of interest to the media and provide another avenue for media coverage of your venue or store.

You can track:

- Retail sales generated by specific special events.
- Number of placements in target media/websites and the relevant media value.
- Overall sales increase year-to-date, which may not be specifically related to a special event, yet can enjoy the "halo" effect of added exposure and increased awareness.
- Number of tourists shopping in your store and how much they spend.

Tracking gives you quantitative results to evaluate your efforts, provide to your organization's stakeholders and even send to the media when appropriate. Think of it this way: Increased tourism is good news for the entire community, so share the good news with the media. When you report, for example, that your French Festival and Bastille Day Shopping Event generated visitation and retail sales at 300 percent over last year, plus drew an estimated 1,500 visitors from across the nation, this translates into hotel stays, meals, transportation and a host of other economic benefits to your local economy. It also reinforces your attraction and store as must-visit destinations for future travelers.

Chapter 6: Action Steps

1. Plan an integrated special events strategy, including both retail and cultural events, as well as targeted tourism events, to provide a solid year-round marketing program.

2. Implement a PR and communications program to support your cultural and heritage tourism goals and objectives.

3. Track tourism numbers and shopping results, and share this data with your organization's stakeholders and the media, when appropriate, to increase media coverage and grow your tourism business.

Chapter 7:
Guest Services—Training Your Team to Be Tourism Ambassadors

> "He who does not travel does not know the value of men."
>
> —*Moorish proverb*

The most effective and frequently overlooked form of travel and tourism marketing is probably right next to you. He's at the front desk, and she's in the store, ready and willing to work with you to build business. Train your customer service team to become effective travel and tourism ambassadors, engaged in welcoming visitors, increasing their spending and generating word of mouth to attract repeat visitors.

"Welcome" Defined

"Gladly received, to greet or receive with pleasure"—from Webster's New World Dictionary

Making guests feel welcome in your institution is a simple, low-cost and effective marketing strategy, both for tourism visitors and your local market. This also is a primary tool to increase visitation and spending in your museum store. Yet, a truly effective frontline hospitality program is one of the most frequently overlooked business strategies in many cultural and heritage destinations.

Look at examples of success in making guests feel welcome in a variety of retail, entertainment and hospitality industries—Disney and five-star hotels like the Four Seasons to name a couple—to see how an effective welcome program and commitment to guest services pay off.

What makes your guests—in particular your first-time guests who have traveled some distance to visit your location—feel truly welcome?

- A warm smile and "welcome" from the first person to greet them
- An easy-to-find and easy-to-use guest services desk, staffed with friendly, helpful people and providing information in languages appropriate to their needs
- User-friendly maps and signage
- Acceptance of credit cards and a convenient ATM
- Restrooms, food and beverages, and the store located conveniently nearby
- Friendly, knowledgeable staff ready and willing to listen and advise on what the visitor sees—and wants to see—at your attraction and in your store
- Free Internet service
- If appropriate, a sign with the word "welcome" in several languages

How "Welcome" Works

I have personally visited hundreds of museums, zoos, aquariums and cultural attractions and have seldom experienced customer service that approaches the tourism hospitality levels evidenced at Disney properties and fine hotels such as the Four Seasons. However, two other examples of excellence also stand out. At Mendocino Coast Botanical Gardens in California, a volunteer staffer served us ice cream in the courtyard café, and then took the time to interact on a personal level and share his passion for these amazing gardens. At the Art Institute of Chicago, a museum guard approached us and suggested that our young daughter might enjoy the free Japanese painting class, and then walked us over to the classroom where it was being held. In both, staff took the time to ask where we were from, interact with us and share their passions for their institutions. These experiences made an impression and caused us to want to return again.

Since you've read this far, you are keenly interested in bringing more visitors through your door using the power of travel and tourism. A simple yet powerful way to do this is to make some subtle yet important changes in the way you and your institution welcome your guests.

In the cultural arena overall, if we are not doing the best job of welcoming guests to our museums, zoos and aquariums, the primary questions we should be asking are: "Why not?", "What can be done?" and "What is the potential for return on investment?"

Why not? Often, managers of cultural and heritage institutions do not focus on guest services or attracting more high-spending tourists. Thus, it's totally understandable that they do a less than stellar job of seeing this need, much less addressing it.

What can be done? Engage marketing and communications professionals whose skill set is about "defining the experience" and ask them, as volunteer committee members or advisors, to engage in a planning process to improve your guest services. Use the ideas in this book as a starting point.

What is the potential return on investment? Here's the best part—minimal investment, maximum ROI. By simply refocusing and educating your current staff and volunteers, and converting this group into your travel and tourism ambassadors, you can reap impressive benefits.

In short, there is an unmet opportunity to grow your business simply by improving your guest experience. The same travelers who are going to pricey theme parks and staying at full-service hotels are also visiting museums, historic homes, zoos, aquariums and other cultural institutions, and are willing to stay longer, spend more and return more frequently if you provide a better overall experience.

Your mission, if you choose to accept it, is to develop and implement a guest welcome program within your organization that will elevate the overall visitor experience and increase visitation and retail sales. The bonus of this tourism strategy is that it works equally well with your local market. It's the perfect win/win situation!

The following case studies illustrate how it's being done at other attractions around the United States.

VIP Guest

I served as the director of marketing for Mall of America for four years, from the ground breaking ceremony through the grand opening and beyond. The Mall of America, located in Minnesota, is the nation's largest enclosed shopping and entertainment center. One of my responsibilities was developing the travel and tourism program. To attract 40 million visits annually to a new attraction in a state with, at the time, only 4.2 million residents, it was critical to have an effective travel and tourism strategy.

We hired a very energetic, young tourism manager, Colleen, who came to me with an idea to print up gold star stickers that said "VIP Guest" along with the Museum of America logo. Colleen suggested that our staff greet every motorcoach group that arrived (more than 3,000 in the first year) and provide each guest with a VIP Guest star to wear throughout the day. She felt this would help the group tour guests feel special. I remember thinking at the time that they'd look like a gang of "deputy dogs" strutting around with sheriff stars, or that they would refuse to wear them, but I agreed to give it a try.

We took this idea to our 400-plus retailers and invited them to become our tourism ambassadors. We supplied the merchants with a simple sign with the VIP Guest gold star symbol and the single word "welcome." The signs were placed in store windows and at the point of sale. We told guests that merchants displaying the sign would give them a discount or a special gift with their purchase, but only if they wore the VIP Guest sticker. Mall of America opened, busloads of guests came and went daily, people wearing the VIP Guest sticker paraded through the mall and business was excellent, although naturally better for some merchants than others.

A few months after the opening, I was walking through the mall early one morning when the owner of the candle kiosk stopped to visit with me. He

had one of the top grossing carts in the mall. He said, "I have to thank you and your team. The secret of my sales success is those VIP Guest gold stars. When I see one of them heading my way, I say—'Hi, I see you're one of our VIP Guests, where are you from?'—and we start a conversation. The next thing you know, they're buying my candles. They love being recognized, and we connect. In fact, I actually watch for those gold stars and make it a point to reach out and talk with those people. It really works."

Are you thinking that a Mall of America example is too big to be relevant to your store? The very successful candle cart is much smaller than a store, and the budget for this campaign—including printing star stickers and signs—was minimal. The key to success was the cart vendor and others like him who were personally engaged in happily welcoming guests and customers.

The First Person

Who is the first person with whom your guests interact? Hoteliers will tell you that one key to success is the right person at the door. "The doorman with the right personality is essential at the front door, because that person becomes your lead ambassador and greeter," says Luis Barrios, general manager of the charming Best Western Hacienda Hotel in Old Town San Diego. "However, even before guests arrive, many will interact with our switchboard staff. They are trained as ambassadors along with the entire staff. The way guests are treated when they call really sets the tone for the visit."

Luis shared a story about the owner of his hotel, a gentleman who lived in Japan and seldom visited. However, as the owner frequently called the hotel, he and his assistant found that one person on the switchboard staff, Teresa, was most accommodating and had the most beautiful and tranquil yet professional voice. As time went on, they always called Teresa, and she connected them to whomever they needed. Needless to say, a special bond developed. When the owner came to visit the hotel, he insisted on personally meeting and thanking Teresa for her superior service. His experience in speaking with Teresa had positively influenced his entire view of the hotel and its operations.

Luis has a global perspective on the hospitality business. He was born in Colombia, has lived in the United States for many years managing several fine hotels and has attended the Disney Institute. In discussing the most important lessons he has learned about training staff as tourism ambassadors, Luis advises: "The two most important things are education and recognition. It is essential to provide in-depth training to everyone who interacts with guests on how to assist guests with the information they need and how needs may differ, depending on whether the guest is a local or a tourist."

Luis continues, "For example, staff must be able to provide information on the trolley route or the hours of a nearby museum. At Disney, they understand that the groundskeepers frequently act as guest services staff so they are fully trained. All the Disney 'cast members,' as they are called, know that when they go into character, whether it's as Pluto or the person selling cold drinks, they have a key ambassador role to play for the entire Disney experience.

He adds, "In addition, recognition is very important to set an example of standards met and exceeded so that others on the team know what is expected."

Another example of excellence in frontline guest services is the bellman at the Omni William Penn Hotel in Pittsburgh. He makes every visitor feel special. This hotel has a rich history of hosting luminaries and celebrities, and a visit with this bellman makes you feel like you are among the rich and famous. In the few minutes it takes to help you in or out with your luggage, you get an impromptu overview of the history of the hotel and its legendary guests, cuisine and more. The bellman, who has worked at the William Penn for many years, is so proud of "his" hotel that guests cannot help but share in his excitement. He makes you want to come back, and he's a terrific ambassador for this hotel and the city of Pittsburgh.

Gail in the Goat Yard

Gail is passionate about animals and serves as a volunteer docent at one of the top zoos in the nation. Gail reports that while the staff is pleasant, there

is no focus on welcoming tourists or any form of hospitality training for the staff and volunteers. This zoo is visited by hundreds of thousands of guests annually and close to 40 percent are tourists. Gail's volunteer training, while very extensive, did not include any mention of hospitality or guest services.

There is a children's goat yard at the zoo. In the goat yard, a volunteer must stand by the gate at all times to watch the goats, keep them from escaping and keep strollers out so they don't get chewed on by the animals. There is no other expectation of the volunteer. When Gail is in the goat yard, however, she uses this opportunity to become an unofficial tourism ambassador with the cheerful phrases: "Welcome to the goat yard!" as guests enter and "Thanks for visiting, have a great day!" as they leave. During her shift, Gail welcomes hundreds of guests, talks with them about the goats and finds that the simple greeting helps them to smile, enjoy and interact more than if they are not welcomed. In fact, visitors will see Gail later in other parts of the zoo and come up to ask questions or visit, because they now know her from the goat yard.

Tap Into the Power of Volunteers

While all staff has a responsibility to learn and implement a successful hospitality program, Gail's experience suggests that training your volunteers as tourism ambassadors and recognizing their success may be one of the simplest and most cost-efficient ways to increase the effectiveness of your hospitality program. Volunteers come from a broad base of experience and typically are eager to support any and all efforts to enhance your institution's success. Most volunteers have the time, the local knowledge and the skill set to be welcoming and gracious. It's up to you to set the tone and the standards by training your volunteers to become your tourism ambassadors.

Key Words That Work

Refer to your visitors, including travelers, tourists and locals, as "guests" whenever possible. The word "guest" connotes a higher level of involvement and more naturally leads to quality service. Refer to guests from other countries as "international guests," not foreigners, which can have a negative connotation.

Refer to your team as "tourism ambassadors" whenever possible. This is a role they will view more seriously than if labeled as "greeters." Likewise, others in your organization will understand this is an important and higher level outreach if you use the term "ambassador."

Where to Start

Follow these steps to get your ambassador program started and running smoothly and efficiently:

1. Develop an official, written "welcome guests" strategy for your organization or, if appropriate, for your store.
2. Make sure all of your frontline people, retail sales staff, volunteers, security staff and custodians are aware of and trained on how to implement your welcome strategy.

3. Track and evaluate the effectiveness of your welcome program and report these results to your management team.
4. Review the strategy, retrain your team and improve on your welcome program annually.

Define the Scope of Your Ambassador Program

Who: Every person who interacts with guests should be trained in the welcome guest ambassador program. Special attention should be given to frontline staff, information staff, museum store staff, volunteers, security personnel and custodians.

What: Develop a team training and education program. Training outcomes should include a commitment to smile and greet guests warmly, and to provide assistance and information to help guests maximize their visit to your institution and the entire area.

When: Use these welcome skills every day. Create an ongoing ambassador program starting with a dedicated training kick-off. Refresher training should be provided seasonally, when new exhibits open, new programs are offered or new merchandise arrives in the store.

Where: Train your ambassadors on site. Information for the training session can be gleaned from internal and external resources, including local tourism authorities who can provide maps, brochures and so on.

Why: Your goal is to reinforce your organization's position as a primary destination for visitors to the area. Train your team to act as tourism ambassadors, welcoming guests and providing the best experience possible at your institution.

How: This concept can be executed very simply is small organizations. Larger institutions will need an integrated team approach at all levels for maximum impact. In all cases, test and fine-tune your ambassador program for the first few months.

How to Develop Your Ambassador Training Program

As with any training program, follow the protocols of your organization. Share this book and your suggestions with your colleagues and then schedule a planning meeting to discuss the program. It's important that all aspects of the program be carefully articulated within the organization. If a similar program already exists, coordinate your efforts to maximize the tourism ambassador benefits.

Next, select a person to research and write your ambassador training program, using the guidelines provided by your organization and those suggested below:

1. Review all information about your organization and its attractions from the visitor's point of view and make sure your team is trained to share this.
   - Summarize/outline key points in a training manual.
2. Gather tourism information and make key contacts.
   - Contact your local convention and visitors bureau (CVB).
   - Contact other attractions nearby.
   - Create a summary "cheat sheet" of all key locations, hours and phone numbers to provide to your guests.
3. Research facts about your local market.
   - Contact your local chamber of commerce and your CVB for statistics and other important regional data.
   - Create regional "fast facts" notes for your staff to share with interested guests.
4. Gather collateral materials to help guests find their way around, both within your institution and in your local region.
   - Review all available maps and collateral to determine what will be most helpful to your guests. Have those items on hand to distribute. Ensure that your staff is familiar with all material and can assist the guests.
   - Provide language-specific aids, as appropriate, when you have or seek to have international guests. Be prepared to welcome and assist them.

5. Set up a system for tracking and rewarding results.
   - Establish a system for reporting on and evaluating your ambassador program. (See guidelines below.)
   - Review and enhance your program periodically.
   - Share your results internally and externally.
   - Recognize and reward team members with a special pin, badge or certificate for completing the training and for ongoing success.
   - Honor a tourism ambassador of the month, selected by a secret shopper from the CVB. This is another good way to build ongoing partnerships with the community.

Tracking Results

Tracking and reporting bottom-line results are essential to the long-term success of this and all marketing programs. For non-gated cultural institutions and those that do not require an admission fee, the impact of tourism visits is challenging to track at the door. However in all cases, the sales impact of tourists on store sales is a key tracking barometer.

Some recommended methods of sales tracking include:

- Fully utilize the tracking capabilities of your point-of-sale system (POS).
- Find out where your guests are from by asking for their ZIP code or country and record this information with the total sales amount. This is a great idea for smaller stores.
- Participate in the AAA Show Your Card & Save Program. This free program provides great tracking and the loyalty of more than 50 million AAA members. The only requirements are that you post a small AAA sign and offer a discount.
- Reward tourists with a small gift with purchase. Simply ask them to show their passport or ID so you can track where they are from. Promote this offer in all your tourism marketing efforts and track the responses that result from each effort.
- Train volunteers to ask visitors to fill out feedback/contact cards that will provide helpful tracking information to your institution. Include

the date, size of group, where guests are from, what they were most interested in, other places they plan to visit, purchases in the store and so on. Instruct volunteers to sign the cards, and then turn the feedback cards into an Ambassador of the Month program. Select one card at random each month and provide a gift certificate as a prize to that month's winning ambassador.

Benefits Beyond Sales

Training your team to become tourism ambassadors has a far greater impact than may be evident at the outset and is greater in many ways than the positive impact on sales. To use an analogy, the effect is similar to taking a course in riding a motorcycle. As you learn to ride the motorcycle, you also become much more aware of all other motorcyclists on the road and how to drive safely to protect them. You start seeing motorcycles where you may have not noticed them before.

The same is true of the tourism ambassador program. You and your team will start seeing tourists in new ways and reaching out to people from all around the world who may already be at your venue or in your store. Your staff and volunteers will be enriched by this new interaction. As they smile and greet everyone, all visitors will benefit. And as they really start seeing tourists, your organization will benefit from a new appreciation of the appeal of your venue to guests from near and far.

Seven Secrets of Highly Successful Tourism Ambassadors

1. Share your local knowledge. Be the local expert who is willing to help.
2. Take the guest there, don't just point them in the right direction. Whenever practical, especially in the store, walk with the guest in response to a question.
3. Solve problems. Be empowered to quickly and easily assist guests.
4. Smile and welcome everyone. Share warm and sincere greetings.
5. Be responsive and helpful. Have the information and tools at hand to assist.
6. Interact with guests by asking where they're from, what they enjoy seeing and where they are going next.
7. Give something extra, such as a gift with purchase for tourists or a special offer to visit another area attraction.

Finally, don't forget to share this information with your stakeholders. Your positive reports will increase their pride in and support of your institution.

Chapter 7: Action Steps

1. Develop a guest welcome program within your organization that will elevate the overall visitor experience and increase visitation and retail sales.

2. Train your team to become tourism ambassadors. This will provide measurable return on investment. Guests will share their positive experiences with others via word-of-mouth, which is a highly effective marketing strategy, and they will stay longer, spend more and return more frequently to places where they have enjoyed a positive experience.

3. Implement a tourism ambassador program that is cost-effective, provides trackable results and is an essential part of a fully integrated tourism marketing program.

Chapter 8:
Driving Cultural Tourism: Drive-Market and Group Tours

With the recent economic challenges, the recession and higher gas prices, there has been increased media coverage of "staycations"—a vacation at home or close to home. While we're all for enjoying the cultural and heritage treasures in our own city or town, clearly the point of travel is, and always will be, to get away and experience new places, ideas and people. In fact, the U.S. Travel Association's "Benefits of Travel" section at www.ustravel.org notes that staycations are planned by only nine percent of active leisure travelers. This suggests that many Americans still plan to "get away" even if their destination is closer to home.

> "It is better to travel well than to arrive."
> —*Buddha*

This chapter looks at research on the benefits of travel, ways in which people seek value as they make travel decisions, and how drive vacations and group tours fit into this context. Use this information to more effectively market your cultural and heritage destination to tourists who drive—whether by car or as part of a group.

Travel Is Good for You

The U.S. Travel Association has been instrumental in highlighting numerous travel trend surveys that outline the mental and physical health benefits of planning and taking a vacation with family, friends or a significant other. Their innovative "Benefits of Travel" data goes beyond the economic benefits of the $759 billion travel industry. Travel provides jobs, contributes to global understanding and has other important social benefits. Data from this research can be used to inform your overall marketing strategies.

Consider these facts, provided by the U.S. Travel Association:

- One out of four American leisure travelers believes a vacation is a birthright (24 percent).
- Even the anticipation of vacation travel generates an increase in positive feelings about one's life as a whole, family, economic situation and health.
- Travelers rate their overall health one full point higher (on a scale of one to five) while on vacation.
- Travelers also get three times more deep sleep after their vacation and sleep almost 20 additional minutes per night after their vacation.
- The Mayo Clinic found that stress leads to a fight or flight response; when unchecked for too long, stress can lead to anxiety, irritability, insomnia and depression. The conclusion: Among other things, Americans need to take mini-vacations from the usual routine.
- Life satisfaction increases during vacation, and these effects continue after returning home, according to a study of employees at the University of Tennessee.
- Rather than detracting from work, vacationing and having a fulfilling life outside of work enhance business accomplishments.
- An inability to take a break can lead to stress, burnout and a greater likelihood of feeling betrayed and angry when things do not go well at work.

For more fuel for your marketing fire, studies also show that there's no better way to break away from the stresses of everyday life than to take a vacation and change your scenery. According to a survey by travel industry expert Peter Yesawich (data also is found on the U.S. Travel Association's website), getting away from home is a vital part of taking a break. He relates that in our fast-paced, pressure-packed, 24/7 world, vacation getaways are more important now than ever. They provide an opportunity to re-energize so we can return to our lives refreshed. In addition, the study found that many Americans feel that vacations are a birthright, and they will plan and save to ensure that they have quality time with their family. The economy has an effect on where families take their vacations, but they will not cancel planned vacations. Instead, families often opt for a closer destination, a shorter trip or search for a destination that provides greater value for their dollar.

Value Is King

Considering these consumer attitudes about travel, it makes sense to promote the benefits of travel as well as vacation options that provide great value for tourists' dollars, including:

- Trips on one tank of gas
- Gas vouchers for an overnight stay
- Weekend getaway packages
- Girlfriend getaways, i.e., women traveling with women to relax and recharge
- Group tours

Value is a key driver. You can suggest many ways a savvy traveler can offset costs. Learn from the examples of hotels, rental car companies, tour operators and the like; they are very much in tune with what drives demand and offer a range of special cost-saving offers to stimulate travel.

Attracting the Masses of Road Travelers

In 2011, Mandala Research, in partnership with Solutionz Holdings, conducted the Drive Market Study to serve as a benchmark to identify, profile and segment drive-market travelers. Shop America Alliance was a co-sponsor of this study. The following statistics come from this research. These numbers are compelling. To develop your tourism marketing plan, it is important to have data to support customer trends and behaviors.

The study found that with 82 percent of the U.S. population taking between one and five leisure trips during the previous 12 months, the expectation to "get away" is almost an American birthright. For 84 percent of those travelers (slightly higher among Boomers and the Silent Generation at 88 percent), the personal car is the preferred mode of transportation—nearly twice as popular as air travel.

The following "car-only" data specifically relates to those who did not use any other form of transportation on the trips discussed. For example, 38 percent of these drive travelers stay with family and friends who will naturally influence where they go and what they do. For these drive travelers, your local marketing and public relations efforts can support your tourism messaging; i.e., "XYZ Museum is the place where locals bring their out-of-town visitors."

According to the study, vacation and visiting relatives were the two primary reasons for taking leisure trips in the past 12 months. Nearly half (48 percent) took a vacation while 41 percent visited relatives. Weekend getaways (27 percent), visiting friends (22 percent) and weekday getaways (15 percent) rounded out the top five reasons. Interestingly, Generation Y (17 percent) showed the greatest participation in weekday getaways.

Higher-income travelers, those making $100,000/year or more, typically cited vacation as the primary reason for their last trip, while those earning less than $50,000 more likely visited relatives.

Distance and Motivation

The Drive Market Study showed that the median mileage for auto travelers on their most recent trip was 299.5 miles with Boomers (310.89 miles) and the Silent Generation (344.67 miles) logging the most distance. Generation Y (244.27 miles) and Generation X (266.57 miles) preferred slightly shorter trips. Nearly four in five (78 percent) prefer driving even when other modes of transportation are available.

The primary reasons for driving focus on convenience and cost. The ability to "stop where I like" was the overall favorite (78 percent), followed by the ability to set one's own schedule (76 percent). The flexibility and ability to bring additional luggage and "more stuff" rated third (63 percent), followed by auto travel being more cost-effective (60 percent). More than half (53 percent) cited "more comfort" as the primary reason. More than 40 percent of all travelers say they like the privacy that comes with driving, and a quarter of all travelers say driving gives them time to think. Twenty-one percent of those travelers 50 and older said it allows them to sightsee along the way.

More than three fifths (61 percent) share responsibility when planning the trip. The most important activities sought on a leisure trip include relaxing and relieving stress (92 percent), creating lasting memories (89 percent), enriching the relationship with spouse, partner or children (83 percent) and trying a new experience (82 percent).

Destinations and Planning

Consistent with all leisure travelers, California and Florida are visited by the greatest number of car-only travelers surveyed, with each state garnering 12 percent of those surveyed. New York also ranks high among these travelers (8 percent), followed by Texas, Pennsylvania, North Carolina and Virginia (6 percent each). The South ranked highest among regions visited with 64 percent. Nearly 70 percent of auto travelers visited urban areas (cities with populations exceeding 100,000). While no city attracted more than 5 percent of these travelers, Orlando was the most visited at 5 percent. Los Angeles, Las Vegas and New York City each had 4 percent of car-only travelers visiting on their most recent trip.

Nearly four in 10 (38 percent) of those surveyed plan their transportation within six days or less of departure, with 24 percent planning lodging during that time period. Slightly less than half (49 percent) plan their transportation two weeks or less prior to their most recent leisure trip. Twenty-one percent planned tickets for events and activities within six days.

More than half (54 percent) of those surveyed traveled with a spouse, 22

percent traveled with other family members, and 19 percent traveled with children under 18 years old. While 33 percent of those under 50 traveled as a couple, 57 percent of those 50 years and older traveled together. The typical length of a leisure trip included three overnight stays, 54 percent of which were at a hotel, motel or resort. Thirty-eight percent stayed with family or friends.

Drive-market travelers use hotels across all lodging tiers, from economy to luxury, with a large proportion using quality tier brands. Only Comfort Inn (13 percent) and Best Western (13 percent) were selected more often among hotel brands than independent hotels (10 percent). The Silent Generation and Generation Y stayed at Comfort Inn more than the other generations. Of the top tier brands, Marriott was selected most, especially among those earning between $30,000 and $50,000 annually.

The majority (71 percent) did not consult a travel agency for their trip. Those using a travel agency (16 percent) did so for arranging accommodations. Boomers, Generation X and Generation Y are more inclined to use an online travel agency or hotel website. Thirty-four percent are current members of AAA, while 15 percent are past members. Almost half (48 percent) of those 64 and older belong to AAA, while 26 percent of Gen Y, 29 percent of Gen X and 29 percent of Boomers are members.

Activities and Interests

Scenic driving (23 percent) and fine dining (21 percent) were the most popular activities enjoyed at the final destination, according to the Drive Market Study. Unlike older generations, Generation Y travelers were more inclined to shop on the way to their destination. Other popular activities included attending sporting events, participating in local culture or history tours, visiting living history museums and visiting history centers/museums (8 percent each).

Eighty-one percent of those surveyed enjoy visiting attractions and towns along the way to their final destination. Seventy-one percent of travelers want their travel experience to be educational and make an effort to explore and learn about the local art. Almost three quarters (72 percent) said learning more about history and local culture is an important factor when choosing a type of activity. Gen Y respondents said this least often (66 percent) while Gen X said it most often (75 percent). More than half of all respondents said that providing educational experiences for their children or grandchildren is an important factor in choosing the type of activity they will engage in on a leisure trip. Among generations, Gen X said this the most.

For 65 percent of travelers surveyed, exploring a different culture is a key motivator in their choice of activities. More than a quarter say that stimulating the mind and pursuing an intellectual challenge are very important factors in choosing activities during their leisure trip, with little statistical difference among age groups. The majority of travelers (68 percent) said that having stories to share is an important factor. Interestingly, younger travelers said this more often than older travelers, 79 percent for Gen Y and 63 percent for Gen X, while only 48 percent for Boomers and those over 64.

For more than half of travelers surveyed (52 percent), seeking solitude is an important factor in decision making. There was slightly more variation among generations on pursuing a challenge as part of their leisure trip. While overall, 69 percent of the travelers surveyed agree with this statement, 79 percent of Gen Y agrees, 71 percent of Gen X, 68 percent of Boomers, and 60 percent of those over 64. Sixty-three percent said being pampered was an important factor in their decision about activities. The variation among generations on whether pursuing a hobby is important was noticeable. While 52 percent of the overall population said that this is an important factor in their decision, it was highest among Gen Y (66 percent), while 55 percent of Gen X, 47 percent of Boomers and 37 percent of those over 64 indicated pursuing a hobby was important.

Exploring nature is an important factor to almost three quarters (74 percent) of car-only travelers. More than half (54 percent) say they are willing to pay more for travel experiences that don't harm the environment.

More than a third (35 percent) indicated that trying a new experience was a very important factor in their decision about which activity to pursue. In addition, there was wide range in responses to whether learning about religion or going on a pilgrimage was an important factor in making decisions about activities. Twenty-nine percent of the overall population say it is important (44 percent of Gen Y, 30 percent of Gen X, 22 percent of Boomers and 21 percent of those over 64.

Spending and Discounts

Generation Y spent the least on the most recent car-only leisure trip (an average of $879), while Generation X spent the most (an average of $1,531). Sixty-two percent of all travelers spent between $1–$250 shopping while 19 percent did not spend any money shopping. Boomers spent the most on shopping, averaging $505.

The availability of discounts, specifically a 20 percent discount on lodging, was noted as having an impact on 66 percent of travelers in making a last

minute leisure trip decisions. The impact of a 10 percent lodging discount was significantly less with 40 percent saying it would have an impact. Generation Y responded most favorably to discounts, with 77 percent saying a 20 percent discount would have an impact and 59 percent responding positively to the influence of a 10 percent discount.

One economic benefit of drive-market travel, beyond the compelling numbers, is the simple fact that shoppers have room to transport their purchases. There are no worries about luggage restrictions or excess baggage fees. Plus the flexibility of auto transportation means that it's easy to visit multiple shopping districts, museums and parks in a leisurely manner and truly enjoy the experience.

Economics and Technology

While economic conditions were the single most negative impact on taking a leisure trip in both 2008 and 2009, gas prices are the factor that impacts the highest percentage of these driving travelers. Almost three-fifths (58 percent) cited gas prices as negatively impacting their decision. Another negative influence is not having disposable income (47 percent). For Generation Y, 40 percent reported being "time poor"—too busy to get away.

Online planning is the preferred method of gathering information, with 63 percent of all travelers going directly to the website of the destination they plan to visit. This is consistent among all generations—50 percent among Gen Y, 63 percent of Gen X and 71 percent of Boomers. Only 29 percent used a traditional travel agency for booking their trips. Seventy percent of driving travelers are likely to use an online website or program that combines trip planning tools for local information about the destination, booking capabilities, mapping and navigational aids.

Conducting general Internet searches using Google, Yahoo or other search engines was cited by 55 percent, ahead of recommendations from family, friends or word-of-mouth (51 percent). Other key sources of information include third-party travel sites at 43 percent (with those over 64 doing it the least at 23 percent compared to 55 percent of Gen X), requested brochures and information at 30 percent (15 percent of Gen Y compared to 38 percent of Boomers and 35 percent of those over 64) and online portals at 26 percent. Ideas from the media, television and movies (23 percent), travel magazines (22 percent), published reviews (19 percent) and newspaper travel sections (18 percent) also play a role.

Nearly 97 percent of survey participants use a computer, with little variance among age groups. Sixty-two percent have a mobile phone, and 43 percent use it on their leisure trips. More than one-third (38 percent) have a portable navigation device or GPS system, and 35 percent have smart phones, with the greatest ownership among Generation X and Generation Y. Five percent of the overall population use an iPad.

More than half of all those surveyed had used social networking sites for two years or more: 68 percent of Gen Y, 61 percent of Gen X, 41 percent of Boomers and 35 percent of those over 64. Facebook is visited by more than half (54 percent) of the travelers surveyed. However, the disparity among generations is quite high with 70 percent of Gen Y regularly visiting Facebook, 60 percent of Gen X, 49 percent of Boomers and 35 percent of those over 64.

Key Marketing Messages

To sum up, these are the marketing messages that will speak to travelers:

- Take a vacation; it's good for you.
- Shop for value; it's everywhere.

- Experience cultural and heritage travel; it's hot!
- Enjoy travel; it's your birthright.
- Drive; it's relaxing

Drive-Market Travel—The Road to Opportunity
Shop America Tours partners with the U.S. Cultural & Heritage Tourism Marketing Council to develop and market The Cultural Traveler packages throughout the United States and worldwide, both online and through leading tour operators. Viewers visited www.ShopAmericaTours.com from more than 170 countries in 2010. To learn more about how your attraction can participate in this opportunity for online marketing, view the current packages at www.TheCulturalTraveler. com or contact the U.S. Cultural & Heritage Tourism Marketing Council.

AAA and Road Travelers

To reach and influence more road travelers, tap into the power of partnerships. (See Chapter 4 for more information.) One key premise is to start with the potential partner with the greatest influence. In the case of drive travel, that partner is AAA, the American Automobile Association.

Founded in 1902, AAA is synonymous with road travel and an influential driver of travel worldwide. As North America's largest motoring and leisure travel organization, AAA provides its more than 51 million U.S. members with travel, insurance, financial and automotive-related services. Here are some quick facts about AAA members:

- Travel more than non-AAA members
- More likely to have four years of college and one or more years of graduate school
- Account for a large portion of the leisure travel spending done by Americans each year

AAA also is an excellent marketing partner for cultural and heritage attractions and stores through the Show Your Card & Save Program. AAA and CAA (the Canadian equivalent) members receive discounts and benefits at more than 150,000 partner locations around the world. Currently, many local museums and cultural attractions are included in the program, but AAA is interested in expanding further. Terry Lindstam, AAA manager, program management and development, states, "AAA members are cultural travelers. We see great value in working with cultural and heritage attractions and their stores, and we welcome their partnership in the Show Your Card & Save Program through our local AAA clubs."

If your organization is not already involved with AAA, this is a great opportunity to expand your visitation numbers and retail sales.

Successful Marketing to Groups—It's as Easy as ABC!

A motor coach takes the same parking space as four cars and has on average 48 passengers. Do the math, and you'll go for the groups!

Most cultural and heritage attractions already have group business, but ask this: Are they the right types of groups, and are you capturing their purchasing potential in your store and restaurant?

Take the time to evaluate your current group business and explore how you can make it more productive. Here are the ABCs for creating an effective strategy to market to the groups that are the most significant revenue generators for your cultural and heritage attraction or store.

A. Identify Your Most Productive Groups

A wide variety of groups may visit your destination, but obviously some generate more sales revenue than others. The first step is to look at all of the group options you have and evaluate those that are visiting now or might visit in the future. As part of your evaluation, determine which groups are potentially the most lucrative.

David Singleman, group coordinator at The J. Paul Getty Museum, says, "The Getty's most lucrative market is the cultural tourist. They tend to be more affluent travelers and more discerning about the quality of the unique merchandise in the museum store. "

Although cultural tourism groups tend to be the most affluent travelers, also consider marketing to conventions and conferences being scheduled in your area, family reunions, school groups, continuing education groups

(including alumni groups), retirement communities and special interest organizations such as garden and book clubs.

Additional resources for identifying prospective groups include AARP (formerly the American Association of Retired People), American Automobile Association (AAA), bank travel clubs, Road Scholar (formerly Elderhostel), the U.S. Travel Association, National Tourism Association (NTA) and the American Bus Association (ABA). Another resource that caters to group organizers is Group Leaders of America (GLAMER). This organization works with group leaders of all sizes and can act as your conduit for reaching them.

As you identify the most lucrative groups as visitors and sales generators for your store, don't forget the special interest groups that support the mission of your institution. Catering to them can also produce public relations benefits.

B. Develop Your Tourism Partnerships for Marketing to Groups

Your second step in your group tourism marketing strategy is to reach out to partners that can help you invite these groups to visit your cultural or heritage destination. (See Chapter 4 for more information.)

Your institution's marketing department is your best resource for identifying appropriate groups and partnering with them on your marketing efforts. Evaluate the groups you both are targeting. Then rank the groups in order of importance as potential sales generators. Next, do some creative brainstorming on ways to expand their purchases in your store.

David Singleman has a very sophisticated plan for marketing The Getty to groups. His plan includes partnering with the museum store to offer discounts on merchandise to groups. He includes these discount offers in his welcome kits, which are distributed to the groups on arrival. He also sends out a bi-monthly newsletter to tour operators and others on his contact list, promoting the museum's exhibitions, shops and services.

David doesn't simply rely on group travel marketing via e-mail and phone calls. He also networks personally with the travel and tourism communities, and other local cultural organizations. Among the travel trade-related meetings he attends are the California Cultural and Heritage Symposium, the International Pow Wow (organized by the U.S. Travel Association) and the Los Angeles Convention and Visitors Bureau's meetings. But whether he attends or not, David makes sure that collateral material about The Getty is at tradeshows and travel meetings. He also conducts familiarization tours (FAMs) for tour operators and travel agents, highlighting the museum's services and the shops.

Groups often are interested in including other activities in their visit. Jeanette Smith, director of sales and marketing at Sauder Village in Archbold, Ohio, meets that need by developing recommended one- and two-day itineraries with suggestions for what to do in the area and posting the suggestions on the group tour section of their Sauder Village's website. She says that they always include the shops at Sauder Village because "shopping is part of the experience."

Another productive marketing partnership resource is your convention and visitor bureau (CVB). Most CVBs have a director of group sales on their staff. Take time to establish a strong working relationship with this individual because he or she is the person who often recommends activities for groups planning to visit your area.

Mindy Shea, director of tour and travel sales for Visit Savannah, notes, "It's extremely helpful when a museum or other cultural attraction keeps us informed on what is being planned at their destination. We are always searching for unique benefits and experiences to recommend to groups." She cautions, however, that the CVB sales team should be made aware of special exhibits or events at least 12 to 18 months in advance because most travel agents, convention and conference coordinators and group tour operators plan their schedule that far ahead.

CVBs often take the lead in creating networking opportunities. By participating, you can share upcoming plans, learn what others are doing and identify ways to work together.

In addition, CVBs host FAM tours to sell their destination to tour operators, conference and convention coordinators, and the travel media. By being an active participant in your CVB and scheduling one-on-one meetings with the sales and marketing team and the director of communications, you will indicate your active interest in hosting FAM tours and increase the possibility that they will showcase your destination.

Also, expand awareness of your cultural and heritage attraction and store, including special services you offer to groups, by providing this information to your regional and state visitor marketing organizations. Many of these organizations attend travel tradeshows and participate in sales missions to promote their constituencies. The more they are aware of your offerings, the more apt they are to promote your group tour services to tour operators and travel agents.

Finally, develop partnerships directly with groups, hotels, and convention and conference centers. Such partnerships have a high potential for generating visitation and sales. By working directly with them, you can customize your offerings to enrich cultural and heritage experiences for their specific groups.

C. Welcome Groups to Increase Visits and Spending

Once you've booked your groups through partnering with your marketing department, your CVB and your own outreach initiatives, your continued success hinges on establishing a reputation for delivering exceptional customer service.

Consider the many ways you can welcome group visitors to your venue and store. One very simple idea is to offer group visitors a discount or a gift with purchase. Here are some additional tips:

- Welcome groups and tell them about the store and dining options as they disembark from their motor coach or enter your site. Ensure that your store is open when groups are visiting your institution… even if it's before or after normal hours.
- Post welcome signs at the entrance, inviting members of the group to your store.
- Encourage staff and docents to tell the group about the store.
- Entertain the group with an event especially for them. For example, have an author's book signing or a demonstration by an artist, gardener or chef. Enriching their experiences encourages people to shop.
- Free their hands by offering to ship their purchases or deliver them to their hotel or motor coach.
- Offer refreshments—something as simple as a bottle of water or samples of foods you might sell, such as a local jam or candy.
- Give each group visitor a complimentary gift or gift bag that includes your brochure, your catalog and small gifts such as a ballpoint pen, logo pin, badge or bookmark.
- If the group is not fluent in English, have an interpreter available if possible. (Note: Survey your volunteers and staff to provide this service.)
- Provide information about currency exchange rates and international size charts.
- Invite everyone in the group to sign your guest book with their contact information. Ask if they would like to be contacted about new products and sales, and if they would like to receive information about special events and catalogs.
- Thank the group tour leaders, not only while they are at your venue and store, but also with a follow-up note inviting them to bring other groups and promising to make their visit special.

Marketing to groups? It's as simple as A, B, C!

Chapter 8: Action Steps

1. Develop value-added promotions to meet the needs of today's travelers.

2. Tap into the drive market to reach an affluent, educated and culturally aware market that accounts for 85 percent of all U.S. travel. Partner with AAA to reach this market.

3. Partner with TheCulturalTraveler.com to develop online exposure for your venue.

4. Cater to and welcome group tours to grow visitation and spending.

Chapter 9:
Riches From Niches: Shopping and Dining/Culinary Marketing

Cultural and heritage tourism offers a wide spectrum with something for every visitor's taste and interest. To effectively target your visitor, you must clearly define and articulate your niche market, e.g., Native American, Civil War, Culinary Tourism, African American, Travel with Kids, Historic Home, Authentic America—you name it.

Why? You are competing for the traveler's most precious resource—time. On a beautiful day, what will make a visitor choose your institution or attraction

rather than another? Effective niche marketing is the essential matchmaker between the visitor's interests and your offerings.

The definition of a niche market is the subset of the market on which a specific product is focusing; therefore, the market niche defines the specific product features aimed at satisfying specific market needs, as well as the price range, production quality and the demographics that it intends to impact.

Niche marketing is not a new subject. In fact, it's used by many cultural and heritage attractions, but not all are equally successful. One of the secrets of successful niche marketing is to have a consistent niche marketing strategy.

Two of the best ways to extend your "brand" and communicate your niche market are through your venue's stores and dining/culinary offerings. Remember, shopping and dining are the top travel activities in the United States, and cultural travelers are shoppers and culinary travelers.

Museum Stores Are a Niche

For example, museum stores are, in essence, a retail niche market, because they are branded with the enviable image of offering quality merchandise that is unique and vetted by the museum. That's why we often hear shoppers say that they love shopping in museum stores. They can find different and unique items not found in traditional retail shops.

Museum stores now more than ever are creating their individual niche— emphasizing that their merchandise is "authentic" to the theme and/or mandate of their museum, striving to offer merchandise that is evocative

of the place or experience, and providing memories of a visit to their destination. To achieve this, they are continually searching for local talent and resources that can provide them with merchandise that supports their niche. With all of these parameters, store managers are also charged with offering merchandise that meets a broad range of price points for children and shoppers of all economic strata and that generates traffic and sales.

The challenge is to make your store more appealing by kicking up your merchandise to a well-honed niche that creates greater appeal for your guests. The interviews and case studies that follow will inspire you to develop your niche in new and innovative ways. We'll look at:

- Juliette Gordon Low Girl Scout National Center
- Pacific Asia Museum
- The Court of Two Sisters
- Biltmore Estate
- Oregon Bounty
- Authentic America

Juliette Gordon Low Girl Scout National Center

by Sheila Armstrong, Executive Director, U.S. Cultural & Heritage Tourism Marketing Council

Charming Savannah, Ga., is the birthplace of Juliette Gordon Low, founder of the Girl Scouts of the USA. Known as the Juliette Gordon Low Girl Scout National Center, the handsome English Regency house is furnished in Victorian antiques.

The museum store focuses on two complementary merchandise themes, carefully selected to relate to the lifestyle of the home and the heritage of the Girl Scouts. Store Manager and Buyer Linda LeFurgy attributes the success in creating this niche museum store to being true to the shop's mission: "to offer a wide variety of high-quality merchandise for sale that relates to the Girls Scouts of the USA, reflects the historic collections in the museum, general Victorian-related products that fit within the stated period in

interpretation, and youth-oriented items that make available an appropriate mix of products for youth and adult visitors at a reasonable and profitable cost."

Linda's diligence in supporting this mission is evident throughout the store, which features early Girl Scout memorabilia and collectibles, including replicas of books and games. There are official Juliette Gordon Low Girl Scout National Center patches and note cards with sketches of the museum commissioned by the store and sold there exclusively.

An especially innovative collection of merchandise is a selection of crafts that Girl Scout troops have created and donated to the museum store. Many of these products emphasize the trend to recycle. For example, there are origami-like change purses that are created from Girl Scout cookie boxes!

The store also has collections relating to the Victorian lifestyle of the Gordon family. For example, teatime is scheduled at the museum in keeping with the era, and the store carries an extensive selection of tea-related merchandise in all price ranges. In short, this museum store has successfully carved out its niche specializing in merchandise that appeals to Girl Scouts of all ages and those who appreciate the lifestyle of the Victorian era, or simply enjoy a lovely tea set!

Pacific Asia Museum

by Sheila Armstrong, Executive Director, U.S. Cultural & Heritage Tourism Marketing Council

At Pacific Asia Museum in Pasadena, Calif., I met with museum store manager Tai-Ling Wong. The museum was once the home of Grace Nicholson, who was one of the best-known art collectors of the 20th century and a great admirer of Asian art. As a result, she built the Treasure House of Oriental and Western Art, now Pacific Asia Museum, "to help introduce Asian arts to a new generation of Americans." The architecture and exhibitions of Pacific Asia Museum reflect the mission of the museum and provide a cultural resource for those who are passionate about Asian

and Pacific Island art and those who have a cultural connection to Asia.

Pacific Asia Museum Store is a reflection of the museum's collection—consistently highlighting the diverse Asian Pacific cultures by featuring the work of both local and international artisans, antiques, and fashionable clothing and jewelry. By focusing on merchandise true to the theme, Tai-Ling has created a niche that is popular with visitors and residents alike who admire the Asian Pacific culture and its artistic interpretations. She finds that shoppers have an appreciation of the quality of the store's products, knowing that they have been vetted by a knowledgeable staff, and trust that their purchases are authentic and worth the investment.

For example, Tai-Ling discovered a local quilter, Grandma Dorie, who creates Asian-motif quilts and wall hangings; a local craftsman, Ken Murano, who makes themed wooden letter boxes; a local artist, Ashley Chen, who creates decorated gourds; and a local designer, Debbie Yumori, who specializes in jewelry designs evocative of Asian themes.

Tai-Ling also imports authentic antique Japanese Tansu chests, some with secret compartments that make them even more interesting. Other examples of merchandise consistent with the niche's theme are Japanese woodblock prints and "singing bowls" often used for meditation. Beautiful Japanese and Chinese scarves and kimonos in rich silks add a fashionable touch to the merchandise selection.

Tai-Ling is very creative in finding resources that are true to the store's niche. For example, she has Asian Pacific artifacts for sale that are on consignment from a former Peace Corps volunteer who is downsizing collections gathered from his travels. No wonder Pacific Asia Museum Store was named one of the "Best of L.A." by *Los Angeles Magazine*!

The Court of Two Sisters

When a restaurant serves up fine food in a historic setting, with live jazz music to enhance the local cultural flavor, it's a special experience. Guests enjoy just that daily at The Court of Two Sisters in New Orleans' French Quarter's historic 613 Rue Royale building.

The Court of Two Sisters restaurant is world famous for its jazz brunch that features a strolling trio playing New Orleans jazz and a traditional Creole menu set in a picturesque old-world courtyard with original gas lights, wisteria, flowing fountains and three charming dining rooms. Some guests have even reported glimpses of resident ghosts at this very special restaurant, providing a new twist to "spirited dining."

Two Creole sisters and the notions shop they owned on this site gave The Court of Two Sisters its name. However, 613 Rue Royale has long played a significant role in the history of the French Quarter and New Orleans.

Originally known as "Governor's Row," the 600 block of Rue Royale was home to five governors, two state Supreme Court justices, a future justice of the U.S. Supreme Court and a future president of the United States.

The two sisters, Emma and Bertha Camors, born 1858 and 1860 respectively, belonged to a proud and aristocratic Creole family. Their "rabais," or notions, outfitted many of the city's finest women with formal gowns, lace and perfumes imported from Paris. Marriage, reversals of fortune, widowhood—nothing could separate the sisters. Indeed, the sisters died within two months of each other in the winter of 1944.

Today, the Fein family owns and manages The Court of Two Sisters. June Fallo has served as director of sales for The Court of Two Sisters for two decades, and is a tireless promoter of cultural and heritage tourism. She has represented the restaurant/attraction as an experience leader on several national and international committees.

On a recent visit with June and her team, we experienced the delicious jazz brunch with a group of travel and tourism colleagues. At the next table, June was hosting a "FAM" (familiarization) tour for a group of Mexican journalists.

"Our marketing strategy with The Court of Two Sisters Restaurant is based on promoting to visitors, both international and national, while also maintaining our local drive-market as a core base of business," June explains. "These groups can range from tour operators and meeting planners to travel agents, cultural clubs, bank clubs and more. The restaurant stands by its true old-fashioned Creole style for both food and the cultural heritage of this original home that dates back to 1832."

June has developed relationships and packaging agreements with tour operators worldwide. With menus translated into seven languages on their website, June took the restaurant international and also developed a core base of locals within a 200-mile radius.

June shares this great advice: "For any attraction, museum, restaurant, etc., we in Louisiana and our surrounding regions work together as a team, not as competitors. Reach out to your neighboring attractions and create a few package ideas. For example, let's say you're a restaurant. Approach the nearest shopping center's main anchor store, present the manager with a great price for breakfast, lunch or dinner, add a museum partner or maybe a historical tour or a local music venue, and promote this package to local and national AAA offices, travel agents, bank clubs, cultural clubs and so on. Then stand back and watch your business grow. You have developed your own network of businesses promoting and selling each other."

Biltmore Estate

Biltmore Estate was the 1895 property of George Vanderbilt, located in Asheville, N.C. The family home, Biltmore House, is a 250-room French Renaissance chateau, the largest private residence in the United States and a National Historic Landmark. On 8,000 acres, today the estate is owned by Vanderbilt's grandson, William (Bill) A.V. Cecil, and includes the nation's most visited winery, a luxury inn, retail shops, outdoor center and fine restaurants.

The estate welcomes about one million visitors annually. It is also a superb example of cultural and heritage tourism, finely honed niche marketing and well-executed merchandising. The Biltmore brand even has pages on its website to promote marketing partnerships.

Bill Cecil, president and CEO of The Biltmore Company, is also their website's official greeter. His online message offers a nice personal touch and sets the tone. "Welcome and thank you for your interest in Biltmore," he says. "What began in 1895 as my great-grandfather's estate continues to be an amazing experience for today's visitors. At its core, Biltmore will always have the natural beauty of the mountains as well as the majestic house and gardens to inspire us and allow us to escape from the every day. Biltmore is still family-owned, and we are passionate about our mission of preservation through self-sufficiency—a philosophy embraced before the first stone was ever put in place.

"We remain self-sustaining through innovation, creative thinking and listening to our guests who continue to tell us they want more ways to connect with Biltmore," Bill continues. "Wine was our first foray into offering a taste of Biltmore. Now, you can experience life as a Vanderbilt guest at our Inn on Biltmore Estate. You can also inspire your own surroundings with a line of home furnishings, decorative accessories, home building products and live plants.

"And so, full circle, we're all about home—welcoming and celebrating family and friends—and extending the spirit of Biltmore beyond our 8,000 acres. It was true in 1895, and it remains true today."

Visitors from all over the world continue to marvel at the 70,000 gallon indoor swimming pool, bowling alley, early 20th century exercise equipment, two-story library and other rooms filled with artwork, furniture and 19th century novelties such as elevators, forced-air heating, centrally controlled clocks, fire alarms and an intercom system.

Biltmore has grown to include Antler Hill Village, which features the award-winning Winery and Farm; the four-star Inn on Biltmore Estate; an equestrian center; numerous restaurants, event and meeting venues; Biltmore® For Your Home, the company's licensed products division; and Biltmore Inspirations, Biltmore's party plan business.

George Vanderbilt probably never imagined that his home would one day serve as inspiration for the development of retail items, ranging from formal china to hand-scraped hardwood floors. Yet just that is happening today with the growth of branded products from Biltmore® For Your Home and Biltmore® Chateau Reserve. Designers from across the United States come to Biltmore to explore the estate, looking for inspiration—perhaps an iron railing or stone carving detail—that will become the next top-selling design for their companies.

Once licensing contracts are signed, company representatives spend several days touring the estate with licensees—visiting Biltmore House, the grounds, the winery, estate barns and other structures. Areas that are normally closed to the public are opened to licensed partners. Results of this process take on every shape and appeal to a broad range of consumer tastes.

At Antler Hill Village, the Biltmore® For Your Home portion of the exhibit includes products from many of the division's licensing partners and hosts demonstrations on decorating and hospitality. There are also computer stations on site where visitors can learn about Biltmore products, locate a retailer in their area and sign up to receive Biltmore e-newsletters. The bi-annually published *Biltmore Style* catalog features partners' products that combine classic design, distinctive style and craftsmanship to reflect the heritage of Biltmore.

Biltmore also works to cultivate the media by issuing the following invitation: "Whether you would like to speak to a winemaker, curator, landscape historian, horticulturist, chef, kitchen gardener or a floral designer, the Biltmore team can connect you with experts in a variety of fields. Biltmore is an excellent resource for respected information on arts, architecture, agriculture, culinary methods, horticulture, winemaking, home products, forest management, history and many other disciplines."

More than a monument to the gilded age, Biltmore goes beyond the exceptional house and garden tour with a clear vision on providing the total guest experience, including:

- Specialty winery experience and free guided winery tours
- Behind-the-scenes guided walking tours
- Biking
- Carriage rides
- Fly-fishing school
- Guided Segway tours
- Guided horseback trail rides
- Kids adventure courses
- River float trips
- Sporting clays school

No tour of the Biltmore Estate is complete without a stop at the most visited winery in America, Biltmore Wines. Long a dream of Bill Cecil, the modern winery grows several varieties of grapes on 94 acres at the estate and produces tens of thousands of cases each year. A self-guided tour and wine tasting is included in estate admission. Afterward, visitors can purchase bottles at discounted prices at the gift shop. In addition, the winery hosts special events and has an outdoor dining area.

Biltmore is clearly in a class by itself in the tourism arena. Nevertheless, its efforts to provide the total visitor experience, attention to marketing details and the success of its brand extension through Biltmore® For Your Home can provide ideas and inspiration for cultural and heritage tourism professionals everywhere.

Travel Oregon's "Oregon Bounty" Program

by Todd Davison, Executive Director, Travel Oregon

Cultural and heritage travelers are foodies, interested in special culinary experiences. Combine that fact with the popularity of annual festivals, and you can reap the benefit of growing visitation and brand awareness. An example is Travel Oregon's "Oregon Bounty" program.

Several years ago, Travel Oregon embraced an innovative solution to a common tourism destination problem: How do we fill room nights and attractions when needed most—the shoulder season? We did our research and learned that culinary tourism was a growing trend. A 2006 study by the U.S. Travel Association found, for example, that 17 percent of American leisure travelers engaged in some type of culinary or wine-related activity while traveling. According to the U.S. Travel Association's 2007 Profile of Culinary Travelers, this equated to more than 27 million travelers. What's more, culinary travelers are both affluent and highly active.

As culinary tourism was emerging, Oregon was experiencing explosive growth in artisan food and wineries. It was the beginning of a foodie revolution unfolding across the state. Artisan producers of all types—distillers, wineries, craft brewers, bakers, heritage pork farmers—were migrating to Oregon. Executives were leaving hi-tech jobs to raise chickens and give cheese-making classes in the Willamette Valley. Stockbrokers were turning into chocolate makers and moving to small, remote towns to pursue their newfound passion.

Further, Oregon's culinary scene is intimate, providing opportunities to enjoy what you eat and drink alongside the very producers who grow, make or cook it. More than a tasting venue, Oregon is a true and memorable culinary adventure. And, as Oregonians know, fall is one of the best times of year to travel around the state if you're a foodie. The weather is glorious and many of the state's best products are at their peak.

The confluence of the emerging culinary travel market and growing Oregon culinary products was auspicious. So Travel Oregon made a strategic decision to have a singular focus for the fall season: Market Oregon as that unmatched place where it's still possible to meet the people and roam the places that make up Oregon's eclectic, hand-crafted, intimate and uncrowded food scene. Oregon Bounty was born.

Oregon Bounty highlighted all regions of the state by promoting events, products, travel packages and local food personalities travelers can meet. The consumer target was affluent culinary travelers, age 25 to 64, who earn at least $75,000 annually and spend at least $1,000 or more per year on travel.

The 2009 Oregon Bounty promotion highlighted eight culinary "personalities" of Oregon, matching each region with an Oregon product and producer. The promotion was executed in the following ways:

- **"Win an Oregon Bounty Cuisinternship" contest.** Consumers entered to win an all-expenses-paid week as an apprentice with a well-known Oregon culinary icon. To enter, they had to post a 140-character "tweet"-friendly statement and a short video on our website about why they were the best candidate for the "job" of their choice. Candidates shared their videos with friends and followers via social media.

- **Launch of a new, comprehensive culinary website**. In previous years, information about Oregon Bounty was available on the state's website only during the fall. For 2009, a comprehensive website was developed to promote culinary tourism year-round (http://food.traveloregon.com).

- **Advertising creative.** Short films/ads, produced in documentary style, followed Portland chef Gabe Rucker as he traveled across the state in search of ingredients for the "perfect Oregon meal." This visual trek introduced consumers to Oregon's diverse culinary landscape and personalities. The films were featured on the Oregon Bounty website, YouTube and in rich media banner advertising. In addition, inspiration maps in large format with whimsical illustrations highlighted both iconic and lesser known food and travel discoveries across the state. Maps were inserted in publications such as *Sunset*, *Wine Spectator* and *Budget Travel* and distributed via "street teams" in wine bars, cafés, bookstores, etc., in key markets. Promotions drove consumers to the website where they could watch the videos and enter the contest.

- **Media outreach.** High-profile culinary bloggers by category (i.e., wine blogger, cheese blogger, etc.) were chosen to judge the "Cuisinternship" contest and were sent an Oregon Foodie Care Package. They were encouraged to share the promotion, their experience with the judging process and their thoughts about Oregon as a culinary destination. In addition, communications were directed to online journalists to leverage the online travel planning trend.

- **Partner outreach**. Alaska/Horizon Air was the official airline partner and offered Oregon Bounty travel packages. Travel Oregon also created a toolkit for industry partners to participate in the marketing program.

Since its inception in 2004, Oregon Bounty has been the strongest consumer promotion ever produced by Travel Oregon. And it keeps getting better. The

2009 campaign survey, for example, showed that 60 percent of respondents were motivated to travel by the Oregon Bounty promotion. In fact, Oregon Bounty 2009 was the most successful campaign ever executed—meeting or exceeding all objectives:

- The promotion generated more than double the unique web visitors in 2009 compared with 2008 (89,903 unique web visitors in 2009 compared with 41,954 in 2008).
- Advertising response rates increased 37 percent year over year.
- The largest single day spike in unique visitors to www.TravelOregon.com occurred (20,000).
- Thirty-two percent of site visitors reported taking a tangible action, such as watching a video, ordering a travel guide, etc.
- PR and blogger relations generated 32 million impressions.

Travel Oregon collaborates extensively with local communities, industry guilds and associations (such as the Oregon Wine Board), government agencies and private business to grow the Oregon Bounty program as a key part of the state's $8.1 billion tourism industry. Partners have opportunities for sponsorship, co-operative advertising, promotion of travel deals and itineraries on www.TravelOregon.com, as well as integrated marketing support via the Oregon Bounty toolkit. With these collaborative contributions, Oregon Bounty has become a marketing engine that drives culinary events and product development to support the state's economy.

Authentic America

A larger niche—and a top travel trend—is "authentic" or "experiential" travel with opportunities to learn, explore and celebrate a sense of place through cultural, culinary and shopping experiences. Increasingly, travelers are seeking these authentic experiences that cannot be replicated elsewhere.

By "authenticity" we mean the local culture, customs and cuisine that result in a special sense of place and the unique experiences that can only be found there—whether "there" is Alaska or Miami, San Francisco or Philadelphia,

New York City or Colorado. Examples include Chef Poon's Walk 'n Wok Chinatown's History, Culture, Food & More in Philadelphia; Melting Pot Food Tours in Los Angeles; and the New Orleans Cooking Experience—all creatively blending culture, cuisine and shopping experiences.

The importance of authenticity is underscored by Ron Solimon, president & CEO of the Indian Pueblo Cultural Center, Inc., and Indian Pueblo Marketing, Inc. Both corporations are owned and operated by the 19 Pueblo Indian tribes of New Mexico and headquartered in Albuquerque, N.M. Ron is a member of the Pueblo of Laguna Indian Tribe of New Mexico and a leader in the travel and tourism industry. He states, "Authentic products and experiences are important to both domestic and international travelers. 'Experiential tourism' requires that tourism venues provide high-quality products, services and experiences for their guests. In addition, this age of instantaneous communications through social media requires that the expectation of authentic experiences, products and services be met in the first instance. If the value proposition is not met, visitors can communicate their dissatisfaction instantaneously to large numbers of people. It is incumbent on us to meet the challenge."

Defining and locating this kind of authenticity can help travelers maximize their experiential travel. This is the objective of a marketing initiative called Authentic America. Promoted by the Museum Store Association, Shop America Alliance, U.S. Cultural & Heritage Tourism Marketing Council and other partners, Authentic America encourages the sale of authentic American products and experiences. Today, visitors to leading museums, galleries, national parks, zoos and aquariums in the United States can discover an inspiring collection of "Authentic America" works of art, apparel or craft created by an American designer, artist, tribe, artisan, writer, musician or entrepreneur as well as items grown or manufactured in the United States, such as specialty foods and wines.

"Authentic America is a big idea that promotes items that are made in America and evoke a sense of place or a unique cultural or heritage aspect of America," states Beverly Barsook, executive director of the Museum Store Association, representing more than 1,600 museum stores. "Authentic America items are unique in their ability to communicate the spirit of an American experience that the traveler can bring home."

International Travelers Shop for Authentic America

According to data tracked by the U.S. Department of Commerce/Office of Travel & Tourism Industries, shopping is the number one activity engaged in by international travelers to the United States. The DOC reports that 87 percent of approximately 60 million inbound international travelers shop. That's more than 52 million international shoppers in the United States every year generating current exports that the DOC estimates at $38.6 billion. These shoppers are also major cultural consumers.

In addition, the data shows that these travelers› attitudes toward travel also predispose them to the consumption of authentic products. For example, nearly a quarter say that when shopping, they find it very important that the "shopping environment reflects the local culture"—a clear indication of their preference for authentic experiences. And their preferences are also evident in what they purchase: Fourteen percent purchase some form of art or crafts in the United States. Food and candies, authentically American products to take back to their home countries, are purchased by 47 percent of these travelers. With almost half of international travelers reporting that they have purchased souvenirs, their participation in authentic, U.S. experiences, their desire for culturally relevant shopping environments, and their high level of shopping spending, there is abundant evidence to support a marketing effort to promote Authentic America goods and services to our international visitors.

Lessons Learned

From all of these case studies, you can distill lessons for developing your own niche marketing strategy. These lessons include:

- A destination "brand" in a competitive retail environment generates higher sales volume.
- Niche marketing builds a more loyal and repeat customer base.
- Addressing targeted customers allows for a more balanced inventory.
- Target marketing lowers marketing costs. (You don't have to create and purchase generalized advertising for a larger market.)
- Compelling merchandising presentations that tell a story increase interest in making a purchase.
- Public relations opportunities expand when the store's spokesperson is sought out by the media as an authority on the store's products.

Chapter 9: Action Steps

1. Promote your unique tourism niche to your target markets via merchandising, tours and events.

2. Target culinary tourists as part of your cultural and heritage marketing activities. Partner with destination restaurants like The Court of the Two Sisters, chefs, wineries and regional cuisine programs like Oregon Bounty. "If you feed them, they will come."

3. Showcase and promote your unique sense of place with Authentic America merchandise and travel experiences.

4. Merchandise your message in creative ways, drawing ideas from Biltmore® For Your Home, Pacific Asia Museum and Juliette Gordon Low Girl Scout National Center.

Chapter 10:
Online, Social Media and Mobile Marketing to Tourists

Nothing has more revolutionized the travel industry and the entire fabric of our society today than the Internet. My father, after he retired from his "real job," enjoyed his fun career as a travel agent and handled my business travel for years. When he was retiring in 1999, I said, "Dad, how will we book travel now?" His answer: "I have one word for you: Travelocity.com."

> "Travel is more than the seeing of sights; it is a change that goes on, deep and permanent, in the ideas of living."
>
> **—Miriam Beard**

This topic is also the most challenging to address in a book because technology is changing so rapidly. Every day there are new digital

developments that must be monitored for the most current marketing opportunities.

From the perspective of the cultural and heritage marketing professional, there are five primary points to consider.

- Is your website friendly and current?
- Do you have an online marketing strategy beyond your website and e-news?
- Do you have a social media strategy and does it support your tourism marketing activities?
- Do you have a mobile marketing strategy that includes an app or mobile-friendly site?
- What is best use of your time and limited resources, and where should you start?

The best filter to review and formulate your interactive marketing strategy starts with an understanding of your target tourism guests. How are they using online and interactive media? How do they get information to visit your location or shop in your store? This knowledge will empower you to make clear and logical decisions.

Make Your Website Traveler-Friendly

Your institution's website is the most efficient way to build important pre-arrival awareness. Awareness, in turn, influences the intent to visit, experience your cultural and heritage assets, and shop in your store.

To make your website work to its fullest advantage, review and refresh it on an ongoing basis. As part of a website audit, ask the following questions:

1. Is the basic information—admission, location, address with ZIP code, phone, hours, parking, overview of collections, descriptions of special events—current, easy to read and user-friendly? Does the website work in smartphone and tablet formats? Are images

high quality? Are store and dining options highlighted, along with location, hours and phone number? Remember, most travelers want to shop and need a place to eat.

2. Does the site have a Travel & Tourism page or section? Are the store and dining options highlighted there?

3. In the Travel & Tourism section, are special offers listed for group tours or individual travelers, such as language option audio tours, interpreters, group discounts, docent tours, special shopping offers or gifts with purchase in the store? Is phone and e-mail information easy to find and use? (Tip: Include local phone numbers with area codes even if you have an 800 number, because 800 numbers are not always accessible outside the United States.)

4. Does the site communicate your outreach and welcome to international visitors? For example, include the word "welcome" in several key languages in the Travel & Tourism section, or incorporate international flags in the design.

5. Can tourists shop your store online? That can be a great source of incremental income. Do you ship? Do you promote this convenient service?

6. Does the website help travelers plan their visit efficiently? They will appreciate knowing what else they may want to do nearby.

7. Are you optimizing search engines? Volumes have been written on this topic, and we cannot begin to delve into all the strategies. Aside from paid links and purchased key words, you can help your "natural selection" at no cost by including key words in the copy on your site, such as travel, tourism, visitor and shopping. You also can link to travel and tourism partners by setting up a page of "Preferred Travel Partners" on your site. Let's look at this important aspect in more detail.

Links and Listings on Partner Travel Websites

Sites with lots of links get more traffic. Once your website is tuned up for tourism, it's time to reach out to your network of travel and tourism partners. Start with your convention and visitors bureau and state office of tourism.

For little or no cost, they should be willing to list your venue and store as must-visit attractions on their sites. Ask if they are open to reciprocal links. If so, place these links on your Travel & Tourism section under "Preferred Travel Partners."

Also link to hotels you work with on packages and other nearby attractions and special events that share similar audiences. Link to local restaurants and shopping centers that partner with you. Ask tour operators to link to your Travel & Tourism section or even feature a video clip about your venue on their websites. In short, use any path that will lead the visitor to your Travel & Tourism section where your store is promoted.

Placement in Online Travel Agent (OTA) Sites

Being featured by online travel agents (OTAs), such as Expedia.com, Travelocity.com, Orbitz.com, UnitedVacations.com, Viator.com, SouthwestVacations.com, GrayLine.com and others, is considered by many to be the key to effective tourism marketing today. OTAs reach millions of online travel shoppers worldwide and can generate the pre-arrival awareness and intent to visit that your attraction needs. In fact, Shop America Tours and its online partners value exposure on key sites at more than $5,000 per page per month, based on what it would cost to advertise.

Fortunately, these sites need you as much as you need them. The travel industry as a whole is becoming much more aware of the popularity of cultural and heritage travel and shopping tourism, and is open to working with you. Your cultural and heritage venue offers the kind of quality that ultimately helps to sell their clients.

Whenever possible, secure your visibility on these high-profile travel sites by offering added value. Net rates, meaning a discount of at least 20 percent off your admission prices, will enable your cultural or heritage attraction to be included in online travel packages. Museum stores can offer a discount or gift with purchase for added value. Even if yours is a free museum, you can add value and be included in online cultural packages with value-adds like complimentary docent tours and headsets.

Tracking Results

As you get your tourism message online and market packages via online travel agents, make sure you track results. Consider the following:

- Integrated marketing is essential. Your online travel marketing plan should be viewed as part of your total tourism marketing strategy, both for the store and the cultural or heritage organization. That way, when you track your tourists at the point of sale and monitor increases, you can attribute the increase, in part, to effective online marketing.
- Packages sold via online travel agents and tour operators should include special offers redeemable with a voucher that can be tracked.
- Your online travel listings have significant PR value that can be analyzed as marketing value. Monitor and report the results of online listings to your organization's stakeholders.
- If you have the ability to monitor your website traffic with Google Analytics, you can track the number of visits to your Travel

& Tourism section and learn which of your links are the most
productive. This is great data and it is free, so collect it at least
weekly.

- Group tours are the easiest to track. If you are engaged in group
business, be sure to account for the size, type and source of all
groups.

Social Media and Leisure Travelers

By "social media," we mean the use of web-based and mobile technologies
to interact and communicate with others. Blogs, Facebook and YouTube are
examples of social media.

Findings from a 2010 study by Mandala Research, "Social Media Use and
Leisure Travelers," are relevant for your cultural and heritage marketing
efforts. The study was commissioned by Heritage Travel, a division of the
National Trust for Historic Preservation, along with the U.S. Cultural &
Heritage Tourism Marketing Council and several other sponsors. Among the
findings:

1. Nearly seven in 10 leisure travelers use the Internet to gather
   information on travel, with 56 percent booking online. Boomers
   and the Silent Generation are more likely to do both than Gen X
   and Gen Y.

2. Leisure travelers represent 68 percent of the U.S. adult population,
   or approximately 152 million Americans. Fifty-two percent of
   these 152 million Americans report that they use social media,
   which totals approximately 79 million social media users.

3. Social media users have a larger economic impact on domestic
   tourism than non-social media users. The total spent by social
   media users ($102.9 billion) is almost 1.47 times higher than spent
   by non-social media users ($69.5 billion). The greater economic
   impact of social media users is driven by the larger number of trips
   they take on average—5.4 trips each year compared with 4.2 trips
   for leisure travelers who do not use social media.

4. The majority of leisure travelers using social media are regular users of Google and Yahoo! and use online sites and tools more than non-social media users.

5. Travelocity and Expedia are the online travel agent sites most regularly used by social media travelers, while there is less differentiation among travelers who do not use social media.

6. The majority of leisure travelers who use social media report a sense of belonging and shared values, and say they enjoy the process of sharing user-generated content. "Heavy" users—those who participate in seven or more social media networks—are more likely to report the sense of belonging and enjoyment from their participation. "Shared values" is also cited as a reason they participate in these user-generated media sites.

7. Social media users are more likely to gather information from websites than travelers who do not use social media. The websites of travel destinations and friends/family members dominate as travel information sources for all leisure travelers.

8. While users and non-users are similar in factors they consider important in their choice of leisure activities, travelers who are users of social media are more likely to want to explore new cultures and history, collect stories to share back home, pursue a hobby, provide educational experiences for their children, pamper themselves and challenge themselves physically. Heavy social media users have higher participation in activities such as enjoying the local or regional cuisine and attending art/craft fairs or festivals.

9. Heavy social media users are more likely to seek experiences that are endemic to the local culture of a destination. They report higher participation in activities such as touring local historic and cultural sites, exploring small towns and urban neighborhoods, and sampling local artisan products, such as cheese, candies, etc. Heavy social media users are also more likely to have shopped at museum stores and to have visited science museums and centers.

10. Heavy social media users are somewhat more likely to tour local

architectural sites and visit living history museums. In addition, a slightly higher percentage have participated in "voluntourism" than the average leisure traveler.

11. While social media networks are getting a great deal of attention lately, only a small share of travelers actually use them to obtain leisure travel information. Excluding Trip Advisor and travel blogs, an even smaller number of travelers consider social media networks dependable. According to the Mandala study, Vision Critical found that among U.S. consumers overall, including daily social media users, friends and family were trusted for recommendations far more than brand-originated content or people that consumers did not know.

12. Despite widespread usage of social media, tour operators are uncertain about its impact on business, with only 43 percent of respondents citing social media as quite or extremely important to business success.

Laura Mandala, Mandala Research, comments: "Our most recent research on leisure travelers shows that large majorities of Gen X, GenY, and Boomers are using social media sites like Facebook. While just about 20 percent say they use these sites for researching and booking travel, the potential for growth for the travel category is enormous. We know from research across many product categories that word-of-mouth is the primary source of information consumers use in making product decisions. Social media expands exponentially the reach of word-of-mouth among family, friends and others that consumers look to for information. At the same time, while we know social media is being used by travelers, we still do not have reliable measures of its affect. For tourism professionals, this means that isolating the impact of their social media investments on any increase in visitation is still a challenge. Social media is becoming a necessary part of the brand building toolbox and, like other elements of that toolbox, it will be difficult to determine exactly how much impact it has on getting visitors through their doors."

The bottom line: People use social media to keep in touch with friends, family and colleagues. They will share travel images and tips, as they will in person or via phone. In terms of travel planning, consumers trust social media communications from friends and family far more than commercial sources. Social media is an extension of word-of-mouth marketing, which is why it can be so effective.

Smartphones and Apps

The cultural traveler is increasingly dependent upon his or her mobile devices, so reaching tourists while they are on the move is a smart strategy. Of course, it's one thing to have a great app and another to get people to download and use it given the plethora of apps on the market today. At a recent tourism industry event devoted to social media, the debate raged on about which strategy is most effective: smart phone apps or mobile websites. The jury is still out.

As reported in June 2011 by blog.flurry.com, "Although the Internet entered the mainstream a mere 15 years ago, life without it today is nearly incomprehensible. And our use of the web has rapidly changed as well. In simple terms, it has evolved from online directories (Yahoo!) to search engines (Google) and now to social media (Facebook). Built on the desktop and notebook PC platform, the web's popularity is significant.

"Today, however, a new platform shift is taking place. In 2011, for the first time, smartphone and tablet shipments exceeded those of desktop and notebook shipments. This move means a new generation of consumers expects their smartphones and tablets to come with instant broadband connectively so they, too, can connect to the Internet."

Flurry says that daily time spent in mobile apps has now surpassed web consumption. The average user now spends nine percent more time using mobile apps than the Internet—an average of 81 minutes daily on mobile apps as of June 2011, compared with 74 minutes on the web.

Flurry goes on to note that the growth in mobile app usage is a result of more sessions during the day per user, as opposed to an increase in session length. Users are checking Twitter and Foursquare more often as opposed to spending more time in the apps during any given session.

In 2011, Flurry also looked at where mobile app users are spending their time. It captured time spent per category across all apps it tracks (more than 85,000). Games and social networking categories dominated, capturing 47 percent and 32 percent respectively on consumer time spent daily. Combined, these two categories control 79 percent of consumers' total app time. Time spent on news apps followed with a nine percent share, and entertainment captured a seven percent share.

Add all this up and you'll see that 91 percent of smartphone users' time is engaged in games, social networking, news and entertainment. That leaves only nine percent for tourism or other apps.

What does this mean for cultural and heritage marketers? Ideally, you will be included on the smartphone apps that your destination, convention and visitors bureau or other partners are investing in now. This inclusion should be free or part of your membership fee. Inclusion in partners' apps also can help promote your organization as a whole. Consider launching your own app only if you have a plan to generate viewership and engage users.

Think of it this way: Travel industry distribution online is largely a numbers game. Place your organization on every relevant app, website or link that your target market may search. More is more, but do so in the context of your budget and where you will garner the greatest results. While the new mobile technology options are amazing, your website remains your primary cost-efficient way to reach and attract tourists.

Chapter 10: Action Steps

1. Audit your website to make sure it is tourism-friendly and up to date. It is your number one marketing tool.

2. Ensure that your website works in smartphone and tablet formats.

3. Work to be included in smartphone apps developed by your tourism partners before you invest in your own app.

4. Watch and learn before you invest in social media marketing; make sure your organization is prepared to devote time and resources to it.

5. Evaluate all social media marketing from a common sense marketing perspective and look for a clear return on investment.

Chapter 11:
Perspectives From Industry Leaders: Innovative Ways to Market Cultural & Heritage Tourism

"Coopertition," defined as collaborating with your competition to reach a common goal, is one of the hallmarks of effective cultural and heritage tourism marketing. By sharing our success stories and working with other organizations—even direct competitors—we can all help to increase the size of the cultural and heritage tourism "pie" and grow collectively as well as individually. The following interviews are shared in the spirit of creative coopertition.

CityPASS

Mike Gallagher is the co-CEO and founder of CityPASS, an innovative company that provides deep-discount ticket packages to top attractions at 11 North American destinations, including New York City, Southern California, San Francisco, Chicago, Seattle, Atlanta, Boston, Hollywood, Houston, Philadelphia and Toronto. Convenience, value and consistency make CityPASS a popular choice by sightseeing travelers.

Prior to launching CityPASS, Gallagher had accumulated a wealth of experience as a theme-park executive and a tourism leader. He started his career in various operations and marketing capacities at SeaWorld San Diego and the San Diego Zoo. In 1974, Gallagher joined Marine World Africa U.S.A. (now Six Flags Discovery Kingdom).

Shortly after he left Marine World in 1997, Gallagher and his friend Mike

Morey introduced the CityPASS program in San Francisco and Seattle. The popular program quickly grew to include 10 major North American cities and Southern California, where the ticket booklet covers admission to Disneyland Park, Disney California Adventure Park, Universal Studios Hollywood, SeaWorld San Diego and the San Diego Zoo. In addition to CityPASS, Gallagher makes time to serve as a leading figure in the travel industry. In 2005, Gallagher and Morey received the prestigious "Entrepreneur of the Year" award from the California Travel Industry Association.

Q: What is your business model for CityPASS?
Gallagher: We're in the business of selling tickets. Due to our extensive sales and marketing, we can do for the attractions what they cannot do for themselves. CityPASS allows marquee destinations to spotlight their premier attractions in a way that draws people throughout the city, while encouraging the use of public transportation. Insider tips advise the best time to visit and not-to-miss activities. Booklets represent savings of up to 50 percent less than if the tickets were purchased separately.

Q: How do you determine what is included in each CityPASS?
Gallagher: The CityPASS concept is simple. Reduced admission is offered for a select collection of the most-visited attractions. In addition, an attraction that may lead a visitor to a new or lesser-known, but equally interesting, cultural experience is often included. Venues and attractions are selected to exceed visitor expectations. Rather than pepper the visitor with a barrage of tickets and mini-offers that will never be used, CityPASS limits its attractions to no more than six per city. Art museums, science centers, zoos, themed attractions and historical attractions are featured, and viewing towers and waterfront cruises are included when appropriate.

Q: You speak about attractions. Does this also mean cultural and heritage organizations that at times do not like to be defined as attractions along with theme parks?
Gallagher: We feature many great cultural attractions in CityPASS,

and yes, we always use the term "attraction" as opposed to "institution." Think about it. Who wants to visit and have fun at an "institution"? These organizations are well advised not to play the "nonprofit" card in the tourism world. They are selling admissions and competing with for-profit, gated attractions, so they need to operate in a similar way. One of our partners that really repositioned and clearly defined how to create a major attraction from what was once an institution is the California Academy of Sciences, the world class aquarium, natural history center and planetarium located in San Francisco's Golden Gate Park. They are very clever marketers, great partners and one of San Francisco's top attractions.

Q: What trends have you seen recently in the sale of CityPASS?
Gallagher: Women are the travel planners and pre-purchasers. We used to sell CityPASS mostly at the attraction partner entrances. Now we sell about 40 percent in advance online and mostly to women planning a vacation. This has grown dramatically in the past three years. I think it's about seeking value.

Q: What advice would you give to cultural and heritage attractions, especially those in smaller markets where CityPASS may not be an option, with regard to marketing to tourists?
Gallagher: First, if they are really interested in tourists—and they should be because local audiences are not enough to sustain most attractions—they need to get involved with their local convention and visitors bureau. They have to go where the tourists are in each community, and the CVB can help them do that. Get involved in your local tourism community. Learn to work with tourism partners and say YES!

Q: How does CityPASS work with CVBs and the media?
Gallagher: In every city, the CVB or tourism office has been an important partner. Those public organizations are essential in communicating with destination attractions, assisting in the launch and continuing to share the message of value to consumers. Depending on the city, CityPASS is available for sale at visitor centers and always at the ticket box office of

each included attraction. In addition, CityPASS is often made available to the media in press kits, providing writers with first-hand experience with the attractions.

Q: How do you define success at CityPASS?
Gallagher: We've created something that consumers are interested in buying. It's a great deal, and it helps simplify the travel experience by saving time and money. CityPASS sales are in the millions. Ninety-nine percent of our customers would recommend CityPASS to others, according to an independent survey of 847 CityPASS users.

Smart Destinations
Cecilia Dahl is the president and founder of Smart Destinations, a premier provider of unlimited admission sightseeing passes in 14 major North American travel destinations from Oahu to New York City. Smart Destinations' Go City Cards and Explorer Passes offer pre-paid access to more than 425 museums, attractions and tours. According to Dahl, the combination of savings and convenience has resulted in a 94 percent customer satisfaction rating, as measured by third-party research. In addition, the company ranked 78 on the "Inc. 500" list of fastest growing companies.

Q: How was Smart Destinations founded and developed?
Dahl: I started Smart Destinations in 2003 after spending almost 10 years as a buyer for wholesale tour operators. During my time as a buyer, I became very interested in the challenges that cultural attractions face in efficiently reaching consumers. While the travel industry was proficient at aggregating and distributing hotel rooms, airline seats and rental cars, there didn't seem to be any efficient distribution platform for cultural attractions.

I noticed three glaring problems in the marketplace. First, cultural attractions struggled to efficiently acquire customers. Second, vacationers struggled to find just the right cultural attractions for their interests. And third, tour operators and travel agents struggled to sell attraction tickets because of the fragmented market. I also was aware of some of the museum passes that existed in Europe (mostly government-owned), and I thought it was a great way for cultural venues to collaborate and provide an easy product that consumers could use depending on their interests. In addition, as a "bundle," it was much easier for tour operators to sell. A great solution! I decided this kind of solution should exist everywhere, and that's how Smart Destinations was born.

My business partner and I set out to automate the passes we wanted to build by creating a ticketing platform that would allow us to tie all of the cultural venues in a destination together into one pass. We built our ticketing system to be expandable and programmable, with the vision of accommodating a number of different product options in the long term. Today our patented, programmable ticketing system accommodates three different kinds of visitor passes: an Unlimited pass that allows customers to do as much as they want for a fixed number of days, similar to a theme-park pass; an Explorer Pass that allows customers to choose three, five or seven attractions from a list of options and take up to 30 days to do so; and a Select pass that allows customers to build their own pass and save more each time they add an attraction.

Q: How does Smart Destinations select cultural attractions?
Dahl: As a company promoting travel, we feel it is important to present our customers with the entire destination experience. We really do seek to include as many cultural venues as possible so that visitors to each destination will have the opportunity to experience not just the major cultural venues, but also the hidden gems. Of course, we are a business, and we do have to factor in our ability to sell an attraction in enough volume to make it profitable for us to include it. Generally, we have found that some "off-the-beaten-path" venues end up being surprisingly popular and tend to be the experiences our customers write about the most in their feedback.

Q: How does Smart Destinations view coopertition?
Dahl: Whenever competing attractions get together and cooperate, it can be

termed "coopertition." I believe that the efficiencies we are creating in this fragmented segment of the tourism market ultimately lead to more business for everyone and at a lower acquisition cost. It's generally a very positive partnership for everyone involved.

Q: Is Smart Destinations an aggregator?
Dahl: We are definitely an aggregator, meaning that we pull a wide variety of products and services together to provide one-stop shopping convenience. Through aggregation and automation, we make it possible for attractions to work together collaboratively, effectively reach consumers, streamline traffic from tour operators and resellers, and automate entry validation, voucher processing and accounting services. We also make it possible for travel resellers to offer a wide spectrum of cultural experiences to their customers while managing only one contract with Smart Destinations. And we make it easy for visitors to access the cultural venues that appeal to them with a single, easy-to-use, money-saving pass.

Q: What trends do you see in marketing cultural and heritage venues?
Dahl: It is becoming more and more common for travelers to not only research cultural venues online, but also purchase tickets before traveling. Like airline tickets, hotel rooms and rental cars, consumers are starting to look for deals at cultural venues as well and will pay in advance to lock in the benefits of savings, skip-the-line privileges or other perks. In addition, mobile technology is quickly emerging as a key marketing tool.

Travel Portland

Barbara Steinfeld has been a trailblazer and leading spokesperson for the important role of convention and visitors bureaus (CVBs) and destination marketing organizations (DMOs) in cultural and heritage tourism. Barbara is the vice president of tourism sales for Travel Portland, the CVB of Portland, Ore. Previously, she was the cultural tourism director there—the fourth one in the country to be hired by a CVB. Barbara has 30 years of tourism marketing experience. She is a founding member and past chair of the Cultural & Heritage Tourism Alliance and a certified tour professional of the National Tourism Association. Barbara is past chair of the board of the Portland Jazz Festival, serves on the board of the U.S. Travel Association's National Council of Destinations, and is on the advisory boards of the Portland Center for the Performing Arts and the Waterfront Blues Festival.

Q: How was cultural and heritage tourism marketing developed in Portland with the CVB?

Steinfeld: In 1997 Travel Portland was the fourth CVB in the country to hire a cultural tourism director. The philosophy was to increase visitors to Portland by using the performing and visual arts and heritage as a hook. In the beginning, the job was to create new collaborations between arts groups and tourism; to educate both communities on the other; and to incorporate the cultural side of Portland into all departments at the CVB, from convention sales to membership to tourism promotions. This philosophy has not changed and is now part of the fabric of Travel Portland.

Tourism marketing dollars were originally invested into cultural events such as Indian Art Northwest, the Safeway Waterfront Blues Festival, the Portland Institute for Contemporary Art's Time-Based Art (TBS) Festival, and the Portland Jazz Festival (which was created specifically as a cultural tourism event). Ticketing passes were designed for attractions and performing arts. Convention delegates were the target of arts postcards touting events in town. In addition, a series of heritage brochures was developed, covering the ethnicities of Portland as well as the LGBT (lesbian, gay, bi-sexual, transgender) market, which started as part of cultural tourism and today is its own market segment.

Q: How are you funded?

Steinfeld: Cultural tourism is funded at $300,000 through a lodging tax to Travel Portland. The system is set up in such a way that $100,000 of the funds runs through the regional arts council to Travel Portland and are allocated to programs in cooperation with the council. Because the funds are allocated through a system of "buckets" that are filled when a certain amount of money is collected, there are lean years when only $200,000 has come into the coffers. That means programming dollars are cut, but the cultural tourism initiative is still alive. Various "pay-to-play" marketing initiatives also are offered by Travel Portland to arts groups. These limited funds are used to offset costs for attractions, galleries and performing groups to participate in Travel Portland programs. We also work with the state of Oregon on the Oregon Bounty annual promotion.

Q: Shifting topics, you helped found the Cultural & Heritage Tourism Alliance. What is it, and what is its focus?

Steinfeld: The Cultural & Heritage Tourism Alliance is an ad hoc organization that was started in 1998 right after the first few cultural tourism directors in the country were hired by destinations. Because those working in cultural tourism came from the arts, heritage and tourism worlds, no other annual conference exactly fit the needs of this group. The idea was to offer an annual networking forum for education and sharing ideas. An informal steering committee was formed to plan the annual get-together, and the group decided to keep the structure informal. We have been meeting ever since, moving from one cultural destination to another, offering an excellent educational program with unbeatable networking. We maintain a website, www.chtalliance.com, and have occasionally been presenters at other tourism and arts conferences, spreading the word about the value of cultural and heritage tourism.

Q: What does the future hold for the Cultural & Heritage Tourism Alliance and cultural and heritage tourism overall?

Steinfeld: We are looking at developing smaller meetings with a more inclusive steering committee. It's almost like going back to the first 1998 meeting. Likewise, we're considering smaller regional events focused on reaching those working in the field.

We have found that the evolution of cultural tourism within destination organizations has often been to be incorporated into other programs from tourism sales to marketing. Cultural tourism is often incorporated into new trends. For example, heritage tourism is a strong element of green and sustainable tourism. Culinary tourism is another hot trend and when cultural tourism is seen as part of it, we find more opportunities for viable programs.

I think the future direction of cultural and heritage tourism is to be a part of these larger tourism trends. I don't think it can stand on its own, but must evolve to stay viable. Visitors are not one-sided; they are multi-dimensional and want to do a variety of activities on each trip. Cultural and heritage tourism is part of that package and needs to find ways to secure its position within the overall tourism message. I am confident that the national message coming from the new Corporation for Travel Promotion will rely on cultural and heritage tourism for part of its international outreach because that is what sets us apart as a destination and gives character to our country. I am not sure it will ever be called "cultural tourism," but it will be present in any viable campaign.

Hargrove International

Cheryl Hargrove of Hargrove International specializes in cultural and heritage tourism marketing communications and strategic planning. She has consulted with more than 200 national, regional, state and local organizations and governments on cultural and heritage tourism assessment, planning, development and marketing assistance. Cheryl organized the inaugural Cultural Heritage Tourism Exchange in 2011 in Washington, D.C., where more than 100 practitioners gathered with representatives of federal agencies and national organizations to discuss strategies for growing cultural and heritage tourism in the United States.

Q: As a nationally recognized expert, you've worked with many communities to help build their cultural and heritage tourism. What do you see as the single most important step a destination can take to market their cultural and heritage tourism assets?
Hargrove: Knowing your customer is fundamental to creating dynamic programs and strategically marketing cultural and heritage assets. Understanding who they are, what types of cultural and heritage activities and experiences they desire, their preferred information outlets and their

trip planning characteristics is vital to creating and implementing a targeted marketing plan.

Q: What is the role of the federal agencies in promoting cultural and heritage tourism in the United States?

Hargrove: Federal agencies, such as the U.S. Department of Commerce/ Office of Travel & Tourism Industries and the National Park Service, provide official research on visitation to and within America. Other federal agencies support or initiate national programs to designate cultural and heritage destinations as National Heritage Areas and Scenic Byways. Some federal agencies also assist destinations with technical assistance and even funding for cultural and heritage tourism development and marketing.

Q: How can a cultural or heritage organization best tap into the resources and services of federal and state government agencies?

Hargrove: Visit www.chtexchange.com for a link to all the federal agencies and national nonprofit organizations involved in cultural and heritage tourism.

Q: What is the best way to measure and track success in cultural and heritage tourism, given widely diverse objectives?

Hargrove: If a site or organization can't hire a firm to conduct tailored research, I recommend working with other entities that are conducting research to meet desired objectives. For instance, partnering with or participating in the local convention and visitors bureau research or research undertaken by a state or national arts or preservation organization can often provide valuable information that is relevant to future development and marketing of programs and products.

Q: What other advice can you share on developing and marketing cultural and heritage tourism?

Hargrove: Partnerships are key to leveraging resources, creating unique experiences and helping others understand your value to tourism and the community. Focusing on authenticity and quality is paramount to sustaining and enhancing growth in cultural and heritage tourism. Defining ways to creatively present distinctive experiences, without compromising the integrity of the asset or information, is also critical to success. Marketing is only as effective as the ability to deliver on the experience.

The Henry Ford: A Case Study on Innovation

If you haven't visited The Henry Ford in Dearborn, Mich., you're in for some BIG surprises. Open since 1929, The Henry Ford is one of the world's premier history destinations and a National Historic Landmark that celebrates American history and innovation. Five distinct attractions at The Henry Ford captivate more than 1.5 million visitors annually: Henry Ford Museum, Greenfield Village, The Ford Rouge Factory Tour, The Benson Ford Research Center and The Henry Ford IMAX Theatre. The Henry Ford is also home to Henry Ford Academy, a public charter high school that educates 485 students a year on the institution's campus and was founded in partnership with The Henry Ford, Ford Motor Company and Wayne County Public Schools.

It is the place where the personal experiences of ordinary and extraordinary individuals, are honored and shared—people like Henry Ford, Thomas Edison, Rosa Parks, Abraham Lincoln, the Wright brothers and others.

The Henry Ford holds 26 million objects and documents including such icons as Thomas Edison's Menlo Park laboratory, Henry Ford's quadricycle, the bus on which Rosa Parks rode when she changed the course of American history and the chair in which Abraham Lincoln was sitting the night he was assassinated

The Henry Ford's mission is to provide unique educational experiences based on authentic objects, stories and lives from America's traditions of ingenuity, resourcefulness and innovation with a purpose to inspire people to learn from these traditions to shape a better future. The institution's vision is to be a nationally recognized destination and force for fueling the spirit of American innovation and inspiring a "can-do" culture.

Patricia Mooradian, president of The Henry Ford since 2005, joined the institution in 2000 as chief operating officer. She has dedicated her efforts to changing the paradigm for what an American history museum can and should be and, in 2001, led The Henry Ford's development of its first 10-year strategic plan.

"At the time of our first 10-year strategic plan, we were in a strong a position to take The Henry Ford, at that time called Henry Ford Museum & Greenfield Village, to a national level," says Patricia. "At the core of our strategic plan was the vision to be the benchmark history attraction in America within the next 10 years, setting the standards in our field for educational value, hospitality and meaningful, memorable and mission-satisfying visitor experiences."

Marketing: A Valued Asset

With a strategic plan in place, an ambitious vision as a guide and plans to create new visitor experiences and public venues, Patricia hired Applied Storytelling in California to assist her team in re-branding the institution.

"We needed to change our language and our approach to doing business," says Patricia. "We had to create the brand words and our own back-story for each venue in our diverse campus. We needed to clearly articulate our philosophy, our education principals, our history, vision, mission and values." To do this, Patricia empowered her staff, which includes 280 full-time and 1,500 part-time seasonal workers.

Carol Kendra is the chief marketing officer at The Henry Ford, and her creativity and vigilance extend the brand message throughout the guest experience. "When we started our branding initiative, we learned from our research that our multiple attractions and their experiences became blurred, confusing visitors with all that we offer," Carol says. "Visitors said they wished they had more time, so our concept of a multi-venue, multi-day visit evolved to help people understand and better plan their visit. In addition, we were finding that internal communication on how we spoke about The Henry Ford was not consistent—how could we expect our visitors to understand us if internal messaging was not unified?"

And then there was the name. In 2001, the entire campus was known as Henry Ford Museum & Greenfield Village, even though the institution had added an IMAX Theater in 1999 and planned to add a research center and a factory tour. The destination name referred to only two of its attractions. As part of the re-branding initiative, Patricia, Carol and the rest of the team changed the campus name to The Henry Ford, which would serve as the umbrella destination name, representing Henry Ford Museum, IMAX Theatre, Greenfield Village, the Benson Ford Research Center and the Ford Rouge Factory Tour.

"It was important for us and for our visitors that we not change the attraction names themselves but lay them out as a complementary family of attractions, each with their own unique personalities," says Carol. "A good analogy is Disney. Disney World is the umbrella destination with many unique attractions like Magic Kingdom, Animal Kingdom, Epcot and MGM Studios. The Carnegie, The Smithsonian and The Getty are also umbrella destination names for a family of many cultural attractions.

"We needed to convey our unique and desirable identity and tell our story to a market advantage," Carol continues. "We created back-stories to paint the picture. These stories and common language not only influenced our graphic identity, but were applied to all areas of operations including programming, food and retail. The Henry Ford was defined as the place that brings the American experience to life, and our branding helped us shape culture,

programming and presentation. Within the process, we also defined our sub-brands or venue brands. To help visitors understand our distinctly different attraction experiences, we needed distinctive back-stories and identities for each venue. In the end, what became really

exciting for the staff was the realization that we were not reinventing ourselves, just clearly articulating who we were. Our branding worked because it was an institution-wide initiative involving all units of business, not just a marketing initiative. The end result not only built brand equity, but community and employee pride.

"We did a slow and thorough brand roll out," Carol recalls. "Part of my job for almost two years was brand training for our 20 units on how the brand applies to each division. Speaking with the same voice, the marketing impact was immediately noticeable with many people thinking we had doubled our marketing budget when in fact it remained the same. That is the power of effective brand communications, and empowering all business units to use the brand. The effort led to a significant increase in national awareness from 62 percent in 2005 to 70 percent in 2011. It also has opened the door for national and international licensing, fundraising and more.

"We are a historic destination, but we operate in the attractions mode," Carol says. "When people make decisions on where to go, the major theme parks have set the bar high, so you have to be competitive. Paying guests will not forgive lack of services or amenities because you are cultural or historic site; they expect the full experience. At The Henry Ford, we are an educational institution, but we can't forget that when people buy tickets for an experience, we are also an attraction."

Hotel Partners and Time Traveler

"When you market yourself as a tourism attraction, with multi-day and multi-venue experiences, hotels are critical," Carol says. "When we first started the program, we had a dozen hotels that partnered with us on a small scale. Now we have a multi-tiered, co-op hotel and marketing partner program with more than 45 hotels, restaurants and other attractions. Both sides cross-promote, creating more marketing muscle for all involved. We visit with our partners regularly, train their staffs and provide tickets so they can experience The Henry Ford first hand. We believe this may be one of the largest tourism partnership programs of its kind in the United States. Part of its strength can also be attributed to sharing research on our impact. Our research shows that 70 percent of our out-of-state visitors came to Detroit specifically for The Henry Ford. This was an important selling feature to our program," she says.

Time Traveler is The Henry Ford's attractive and informative annual magazine. First created to communicate The Henry Ford as a destination for group tours and fully explain the many diverse offerings, *Time Traveler* has evolved to include all the hotel and marketing partners, including the Detroit Tigers, Delta Airlines and even Buddy's, a local pizza restaurant. Distributed nationally to tour operators, regionally to high traffic venues like doctor's offices and to the 40,000 members of The Henry Ford, *Time Traveler* is an impressive marketing tool with a circulation of more than 100,000.

Enhancing the Visitor Experience

The Henry Ford had, for many years, experienced a seasonal decline in business, as is typical for many museums. In an effort to showcase the institution's expertise regarding holiday traditions while attracting the built-in audience of tourists to Michigan during the holiday season, the team developed "Holiday Nights," a 12-night festival that invited guests to step back in time and enjoy authentic food, costumed carolers, ice skating, holiday home tours down lantern-lit paths, and carriage and Model T rides. The attendance grew from 15,000 the first year to more than 60,000 with USA Today naming The Henry Ford Holiday Nights as one of the "Top Ten Holiday Things To Do."

The award-winning food service and catering operations at The Henry Ford employ some of the nation's finest chefs who are committed to using a consortium of regional farmers and historical recipes. Special events for corporate groups and weddings are a major business at The Henry Ford and have more than doubled in the past five years due to a commitment to quality and effective marketing.

Retail sales at The Henry Ford also benefit from a strong in-house oversight of national retail sales, licensed products and highly skilled artisans. The Henry Ford has eight retail shops, including one at Detroit International Airport, along with seasonal carts and kiosks. The merchandise philosophy focuses on items that are unique and reflective of The Henry Ford's deep American roots, but with modern themes appropriate to contemporary lifestyles.

Today, 10 years later, The Henry Ford continues to hone its product offerings, visitor experiences and brand. In 2010, the institution took its vision to the next level and developed Vision 2020, its strategic plan for the next 10 years.

Vision 2020 begins with a new vision statement: "The Henry Ford will be a nationally recognized destination and force for fueling the spirit of American innovation and inspiring a 'can-do' culture."

"This vision suggests national, top-of-mind awareness for The Henry Ford," says Patricia. "It says we will always be a major destination and attraction, but it also says we're going to new levels to rekindle, instill, stimulate and inspire the very spirit that lives in the DNA of America—the spirit of innovation—and the can-do kind of attitude that is the foundation for creativity, imagination and the entrepreneurial essence of America's people. It's the spirit that's embedded in the lives of the heroes that live on at The Henry Ford. It's the past that gives meaning to the present and inspires the future."

To accomplish this vision, The Henry Ford will focus on four key strategies:

- Innovation
- Collections and access
- Community engagement and educational experiences
- New earned and contributed revenue

With this plan firmly in place and goals relating to relevance, sustainability, community impact and national awareness, The Henry Ford aspires to be the on-site, off-site and virtual go-to resource for the contemporary and past stories of innovation, resourcefulness and ingenuity. Its collections, expertise and educational content will be readily accessible online and through other technology applications. They intend to co-create virtual experiences that will help develop new relationships with new audiences that further The Henry Ford's role as one of America's greatest history attractions.

Chapter 11: Action Steps

1. Embrace the art of coopertition (cooperating with your competitors) to enhance your success in tourism marketing.

2. Work with an attractions aggregator like CityPASS or Smart Destinations, when possible depending on your market, to be included in their multiple-venue passes and sophisticated tourism marketing.

3. Check out government resources for data and possible grant funding. Visit www.chtexchange.com and www.tinet.ita.doc.gov.

4. Innovate and redefine your organization, as The Henry Ford has, to build tourism into your long-term 'can-do' vision.

Chapter 12:
Developing Your Cultural & Heritage Tourism Marketing Plan With a Focus on Innovation and Cultural Entrepreneurship

Throughout this book we've shared ideas, perspectives, case studies and information that can help you to increase your visitation and retail business through incremental cultural and heritage tourism. To significantly grow tourism, however, it's essential to formalize a tourism marketing plan as part of your overall marketing plan. A written strategic plan is the number one tool for marketing success. "Write it down, make it happen" is the golden rule here. If writing is not your thing, start with a simple outline of bullet points. Get your plan into a document that is easy to edit, update and share.

Writing a tourism marketing plan can be intimidating, but you can do it. The guidelines found in this chapter will help, and several approaches are

presented. But equally important is to keep in mind that your ideas, program and plans must flow from realistic expectations and make sense to everyone on your team.

A Tourism Marketing Plan Outline

Use the following steps as a guide to developing your cultural and heritage tourism marketing plan:

1. Complete a situation analysis, including your current level of tourism and positioning, and opportunities for growth through investment or partnerships.
2. Quantify business goals and objectives.
3. Do a SWOT analysis. (See sidebar.)
4. Review and reference research, either found in this book or elsewhere, to assist you in developing your marketing plan.
5. Identify your resources, budget and potential partners.
6. Outline who will do what, including your team, staff, volunteers and partners.
7. Create a realistic timeline with milestones.
8. Build in tracking and measurement systems as appropriate: ZIP code surveys, Google Analytics, media release pick-up, partnership revenue, and incremental arrivals and sales.
9. Reach out for third-party endorsement or counsel.

SWOT Self-Analysis Survey
A good way to begin developing a tourism marketing plan is with a SWOT analysis—an analysis of your organization's strengths, weaknesses, opportunities and threats. When looking at strengths, consider that each individual contributes to the goals and objectives of an organization in unique ways. To better evaluate the internal strengths and weaknesses of the organization, as well as the broader external opportunities and threats facing the destination, convene a visioning or strategic planning session and ask each participant to complete the following questionnaire. This also will help you better understand the attitudes and interests of each participant.

1. In 15 words or less, describe your current cultural or heritage destination and organization.
2. What do you consider your organization's key strengths?
3. What do you consider your organization's major weaknesses?
4. What do you consider the greatest cultural or heritage tourism opportunities for your destination?

---

5. What do you consider the greatest challenges for your destination?
6. Why are you interested or involved in the destination/organization?
7. How do you currently contribute to your organization's vision?
8. What role would you like to play in your organization in five years?
9. What tools, training or professional development opportunities are necessary to reach your destination's five-year goal in cultural and heritage tourism?
10. What measurable result would you like to help your destination accomplish in the next 18 months?

Two helpful websites to assist you are www.culturalheritagetourism.org and www.preservationnation.org/survival-toolkit. Both are managed by the National Trust for Historic Preservation and provide resources for organizations and individuals who are developing, marketing or managing cultural and heritage tourism attractions or programs. The information that follows is from www.culturalheritagetourism.org and is shared with permission. Visit the site for more case studies and tourism tools.

The National Trust for Historic Preservation's Heritage Tourism Program
Amy Jordan Webb is director of the Heritage Tourism Program for the National Trust for Historic Preservation. Amy joined the National Trust for Historic Preservation's Heritage Tourism Program in 1993 and has served as the program's director since 1995. She has authored two cultural and heritage tourism success stories, and has developed online resources including a how-to website for practitioners at www.culturalheritagetourism.org and a cultural heritage tourism survival toolkit at www.preservationnation.org/survival-toolkit.

Amy explains: "This site has been developed as a resource for organizations and individuals who are developing, marketing or managing cultural and heritage tourism attractions or programs. These cultural and heritage tourism 'practitioners' can come from a variety of fields—tourism, historic preservation, the arts, humanities, museums, economic development, Main Street, heritage areas and many other fields. Practitioners can include nonprofit organizations, government entities, federal agencies and coalitions formed to bring these and other partners together. While the variety of partners contributes to the richness of cultural and heritage tourism, it can also make it more difficult to track down resources and how-to information."

Basic Principles for Tourism Planning

The following principles, provided by the National Trust for Historic Preservation, can help you make the most of your opportunities for marketing cultural and heritage tourism.

1. Collaborate
Much more can be accomplished by working together than by working alone. Successful cultural and heritage tourism programs bring together partners who may not have worked together in the past.

Building partnerships is essential, not just because they help develop local support, but also because tourism demands resources that no single organization can supply. Its success depends on the active participation of political leaders, business leaders, operators of tourist sites, artists and craftspeople, hotel/motel operators, and many other people and groups. Regional partnerships also are useful to cultural and heritage tourism efforts. Cooperating in a regional arrangement lets you develop regional themes, pool resources, save money and expand your marketing potential. Those resources include not only money for marketing campaigns, for example, but also facilities (accommodations for travelers, for example) or expertise in tourism, preservation, the arts or another area.

2. Find the Fit
Balancing the needs of residents and visitors is important to ensure that cultural and heritage tourism benefits everyone. It is important to understand the kind and amount of tourism that your community can handle.

Local priorities vary. So do local capabilities. In other words, local circumstances determine what your area needs to do and can do in cultural and heritage tourism. Programs that succeed have widespread local acceptance and meet recognized local needs. They also are realistic, based on the talents of specific people as well as on specific attractions, accommodations, and sources of support and enthusiasm.

One of the reasons cultural and heritage tourism is on the rise in the United States is that travelers are seeking out experiences that are distinctive, not homogenized. They want to get the feel of a very particular place or time.

You can supply that experience and benefit in the process—but only if your cultural and heritage tourism program is firmly grounded in local circumstances. Ask the following questions:

- Do the residents of your area want tourism?
- Why do they want it?
- Are there certain times of year or certain places they do not want to share?
- How will tourism revenues improve life in your area and affect services such as fire and police protection?
- What is the maximum number of cars or buses your area can handle? On roads? In parking lots?
- Can you accommodate group tours? Do sites accommodate at least 40 people at once with amenities such as restrooms, snacks and a seating area?
- Can you accommodate visitors with disabilities or special needs?

3. Make Sites and Programs Come Alive
Competition for time is fierce. To attract visitors, you must be sure that the destination is worth the drive. The human drama of history is what visitors want to discover, not just names and dates. Interpreting sites is important, and so is making the message creative and exciting. Find ways to engage as many of the visitor's five senses as you can, as the more senses are involved, the more visitors will retain. On average, visitors will remember: 10 percent of what they hear, 30 percent of what they read, 50 percent of what they see and 90 percent of what they do.

4. Focus on Quality and Authenticity
Quality is an essential ingredient for all cultural and heritage tourism, and authenticity is critical whenever heritage or history is involved. The true story of your area is the one worth telling. The story of the authentic contributions previous generations have made to the history and culture of where you live is the one that will interest visitors, because that is what distinguishes your area from every other place on earth. It is authenticity

that adds real value and appeal. Your area is unique, and its special charm is what will draw visitors. By doing the job right—by focusing on authenticity and quality—you give your area the edge.

5. Preserve and Protect

A community's cultural, historic and natural resources are valuable and often irreplaceable. As a good look around almost any city or town will show, people are often tempted to provide a quick fix—a "band-aid" solution—to cover up an old storefront inexpensively, for example, rather than to restore it. But when your historic and cultural assets are at the heart of your plans to develop tourism, it's essential to protect them for the long term.

Hearts break when irreplaceable structures are destroyed or damaged beyond repair, instead of preserved and protected as they deserve. A plaque pointing out "on this site a great building once stood" can't tell that story. Equally tragic is the loss of traditions: a way of crafting wood or farming, of celebrating holidays or feasting on "old world" cuisine. The preservation and perpetuation of traditions are important to telling the story of the people who settled the land. By protecting the buildings, landscape or special places and qualities that attract visitors, you safeguard the future.

Five Steps to an Effective Marketing Plan

By Thomas H. Aageson, Executive Director, Global Center for Cultural Entrepreneurship

Tom Aageson is executive director of the Global Center for Cultural Entrepreneurship. He co-founded GCCE with the mission to mentor cultural entrepreneurs and strengthen their cultural enterprises.

Aageson served for nine years as executive director of the Museum of New Mexico Foundation in Santa Fe, N.M. The Foundation provides private support to the Museum of New Mexico's (MNM) four museums and six state monuments. The Foundation earns and raises private operating, capital and endowment funds, operates a membership program of 6,500 households, and manages six museum shops and a national licensing program—all for the benefit of the MNM. During his tenure, the Shape the Future campaign raised $25 million.

Aageson led the development of New Mexico Creates, an award-winning economic development initiative that markets the work of New Mexico artists and artisans in museum shops and online, and co-founded the Santa Fe International Folk Art Market. A cultural entrepreneur, Aageson also created the successful Maritime Art Gallery at Mystic Seaport Museum in Mystic, Conn., along with a print and book publishing venture, Mystic Maritime Graphics.

A marketing plan is built in five steps:

1. Situation analysis
2. Determining market opportunity
3. Setting marketing objectives
4. Strategy and program development
5. Implementation, monitoring, evaluation

I would like to caution that you cannot begin to plan before you answer this basic question: What kind of experience does your venue offer to visitors? The answer is not an inventory of your holdings, but a description of the activities the visitor can enjoy. For example, a museum might have 10,527 paintings, sculptures and prints in its collection. Perhaps there are five galleries, and two new exhibitions are scheduled in the coming year. Unfortunately, such a shopping list of assets will mean little to your potential customer. Instead, describe the collection in terms of the experience: "The visitor will view seven previously unseen artworks by Andrew Wyeth; together, they explain how he created his most famous painting, 'Christina's World.'" Or, "This new exhibit will put visitors behind a printmaking press, where they can experience the world of the artist at work."

1. Situation Analysis

Situation analysis is the first step in developing a strategic marketing plan. Surveying your attraction's current context in terms of its marketplace lays the groundwork for the future.

First, find out about your current customers. This is best answered by market research. Asking visitors for their ZIP codes, for example, can reveal a great deal about who visits during different periods of the year. Conduct an analysis that attempts to answer the following questions: Why do visitors come? Who makes the decision to visit? When do visitors make the decision? The answers to these questions are very important because they can tell management where and when to market.

Also review how various societal values influence visitor attendance. For example, is attending a children's or science museum a family-driven decision? If a focus group session reveals that mothers influence the decision to attend your attraction, the promotion strategy should be focused on reaching those decision-makers.

Next, review the political environment. How is local, state or national legislation affecting your organization? For example, funding issues at the National Endowment for the Arts may change exhibit schedules. An effort to tax admissions might affect pricing. New arts legislation might free up marketing dollars. Or funds for marketing a future exhibit might be available from a new state tourism grants program.

In addition, assess the economic environment. Economic upturns and downturns will influence attendance, as will changes in the interest rate or regional changes in employment. Gas prices can change travel patterns. Families with two working parents may not have a lot of time to spend at your venue. Rising marketing costs may seriously affect your budget.

Also identify your competition, which can be very broad. Competition for people's time—rather than for their money—is often the most serious obstacle to success. What other attractions are targeting your potential visitors? Knowing the answer to this question will lead to important marketing decisions.

The physical environment likewise determines how you structure a marketing plan. Pay attention to seasonal influences. Are there changing weather patterns in your area? Factors like location, terrain of the site, accessibility, parking and public transportation will affect the plan.

Technology plays an essential role in marketing plans as well. How will technology impact your attraction today and in the future? How can online traffic or social media friends translate into more visitors on site? Evaluate your advertising promotions by tracking the time of arrival and origin of online visits. Engage the guest to allow efficient follow-up e-marketing, which helps develop a relationship with the visitor.

Continue to analyze your institution's situation while you carry out the plan. Audit your marketing campaigns on a regular basis. The marketing audit will point to the strengths and weaknesses of your plan. Examine policies, structure, staff, resources and objectives. Evaluate current marketing objectives, determine whether goals have been met and assess the reasons for the results. In short, have you reached your target audience?

2. Market Opportunity
After examining the current situation and the external influences on attendance, determine your potential audience. Look beyond the traditional market. For example, if ZIP code data shows that residents in a major metropolitan area do not visit, concentrate marketing efforts in that metro area during the coming year. Focus groups with non-visitor participants will tell you whether your exhibit and program concepts will motivate them to visit.

Decide if there are new markets you want to attract. Then narrow the list by targeting key markets because resources will be limited. It is better to concentrate your budget than to dilute efforts over several markets. Separate markets by various categories, such as interests, age, season, geography, psychographic or demographic descriptors. This information can be derived in part from ZIP code analysis.

Each audience segment or niche is unique, whether families, school groups, senior citizens, ethnic groups or tourists. Visitor surveys will help to identify your customer segments in terms of where they live, when they visit and why they visit. The goal is to clearly define your target audience for each year's plan.

3. Setting Market Objectives

Begin with basic, broad objectives. State the overall attendance and revenue goal, and then break each into market segments. Spell out marketing initiatives that are critical and unique to the plan, such as promotions in a new market, marketing collaborations with local businesses or a special exhibit. Mention new initiatives such as building alliances with other venues or testing combination ticketing.

Then get specific: What's the deadline for achieving various goals? Establish monthly and quarterly action plans. State figures for the attendance and revenue goals you plan to achieve by the deadline. Determine how you plan to reach your target audience.

4. Strategy and Program Development

To develop the means for carrying out the plan, return to the "visitor experience" mentioned previously. Based on the experience offered by your venue and the profile of its customers, determine how you will present the institution to the public. First, develop a positioning statement. This is where the institution's mission and its marketing come together, and everyone in senior management can agree on the statement. This is the key message that will create a lasting impression on people.

Once the marketing position is established, address the essential elements of the marketing mix: product, price, promotion and place. Product is the description of what the organization will offer to the visitor during the coming year. The best way to describe programs and exhibits is through the experience that they create for the visitor. For example, a program featuring rural basket makers at a natural history museum is best described in terms of the experience the visitor will have interacting with the objects and meeting the artisans. Stress the benefits to the visitor.

Next comes the pricing strategy. Visitors have an inner calculator that tells them if their visit will be worth the price. The would-be customer balances the perceived benefits against the price and the time available for a visit. Setting prices is very important, and the pricing strategy must be clear, especially in this era of online marketing and extreme value sensitivity.

Promotion is what people often think of as marketing, yet it is only part of the mix. It includes website, advertising, public relations, events and sales of activities such as group tours. Marketing staff defines the creative strategy that is built on the positioning statement. The creative strategy includes developing artwork for print and TV, headlines and copy for print ads, and identifying the "voice" for radio and TV ads. Promotion staff develops the rough layouts of the ads, considering such elements as the copy and type. Public relations is best developed with the marketing plan and supports the strategic direction, audience-segmentation decision, market position and creative plan. Also known as publicity, public relations will reinforce all of the marketing work and is part of the promotion effort.

After you develop the creative strategy, establish a monthly schedule for ads, online marketing, social media, brochures and special promotions. Allocate funds for brochures, print ads, radio, TV, outdoor advertising and online/social media at this stage. Your choice of medium should be based on the demographics of your potential customers, and when and where they make their leisure decisions. For example, if you want to reach out-of-town visitors, place ads in regional and state publications that travelers read. If your venue is a destination chosen by local families a week or less before they arrive, promote the institution in the local media. Choosing the appropriate medium for your message requires a great deal of preparation. Some special events require tickets and therefore take a longer time to promote. Other events may benefit from heavy promotion closer to opening day.

The fourth part of the marketing mix is "place," or where distribution of the product occurs. Marketing planning must address issues of signage, arrival points, access to the attraction, the impact of the entrance and potential events at other locations.

Next, develop the budget, which should include staff salaries, costs of advertising, ad preparations, brochures and their distribution, mailing costs, processing of brochure requests, special event expenses, participation in tradeshows and market research. Give special attention to your online and social media needs and budgets. No organization will have enough money to do all the marketing it feels is required to build audiences. But, as hard as it is to allocate limited resources, managers will be more confident if they base decisions on good research and solid planning.

Market research is essential for understanding your audience and how it changes, and for measuring the effectiveness of the promotional campaign. In your annual budget, allocate funds for gathering data that will be used to fine tune next year's plan. Many institutions dedicate five percent of their marketing budget to research.

5. Implementation, Monitoring and Evaluation
The entire institution must buy into the marketing plan, from the board to the director to the staff. Well-informed staff members can be enthusiastic supporters of the plan.

To monitor performance, place objectives in the marketing plan. Objectives can include attendance, revenues, media coverage, web traffic, social media connections, research schedules, special events and market tests. These objectives should be reported on a quarterly basis at least. Most institutions track attendance and revenue daily.

How does your store and food service fit into the marketing plan? Both store and food service management should be brought into the planning very early. They, in turn, should be asked to develop their own annual business plans, taking the main marketing plan into consideration. Other profit centers, such as photo rights, publications and licensing, also need their own plans. These, too, must dovetail with the overall marketing plan.

At the end of the year, conduct a formal evaluation by comparing the marketing plan objectives with the results achieved. Assess in depth how your strategies worked. Report on the market research and the test conclusions. Think of the evaluation as the end of this year›s plan and the beginning of next year's plan. Thus, the planning cycle gains a rhythm. The next plan will be more refined and the process more trusted.

Cultural Entrepreneurs: Producing Cultural Value and Wealth
By Thomas Aageson

Cultural entrepreneurs are change agents who leverage cultural innovation to create thriving economic systems. They are resourceful visionaries who take risks and generate revenues from cultural activities; their innovative applications of traditions to markets result in economically sustainable cultural enterprises. These enterprises enhance livelihoods and create cultural value for both creative producers and consumers of cultural services and products.

At the Global Center for Cultural Entrepreneurship we envision a world in which cultural entrepreneurship creates cultural value and wealth, self-determination, and cultural diversity in communities across the globe. We envision a world in which cultural entrepreneurs are catalysts for cultural innovation through their cultural enterprises. Toward this vision, we are creating the world's first networked community of cultural entrepreneurs, cultural investors and cultural entrepreneurship educators.

To learn more, please visit www.culturalentrepreneur.org.

Chapter 12: Action Steps

1. Conduct a SWOT analysis as part of your tourism marketing plan.

2. Follow the National Trust for Historic Preservation's five principles for tourism planning and view their website for other helpful tools.

3. Integrate your tourism marketing plan with your organization's overall marketing plan using guidelines outlined in this chapter.

4. Incorporate marketing efforts into all aspects of the organization to maximize the guest experience.

5. Think big, work smart, grow wisely and be an innovator and a cultural entrepreneur.

Conclusion and Acknowledgements

This is not the end! It is the beginning of new opportunities for everyone who embraces marketing cultural and heritage tourism as a national and international movement. Innovative thinking and cultural entrepreneurship are the prevailing themes of this book. It's up to you to use these tools and write the next chapters in "Marketing Cultural & Heritage Tourism."

I have been inspired by and am indebted to many cultural and heritage tourism success stories, research studies and perspectives. I would like to acknowledge in particular: Patricia Mooradian and Carol Kendra with The Henry Ford; Laura Mandala with Mandala Research; Pat Lee with Pat Lee & Associates; the American Automobile Association; Chicke Fitzgerald with Solutionz; American Express; Rick Still; Brad Weber at Gray Line Worldwide; Luis Barrios at Best Western Hacienda San Diego; Helen Marano, Julie Heizer and Ron Erdmann at the U.S. Department of Commerce/Office of Travel & Tourism Industries; Roger Dow and his great team at the U.S. Travel Association; Biltmore Estates; Todd Davidson with Travel Oregon; Mike Gallagher with CityPASS; Cecilia Dahl with Smart Destinations; Ron Solimon with Indian Pueblo Cultural Center; June Fallo with The Court of Two Sisters; City of Chicago Cultural Affairs; Juliette Gordon Low Girl Scout National Center; David Singleman with The Getty; Mindy Shea with Visit Savannah; Nancy Hahn Bono with Visit Orlando; Chef Poon in Philadelphia; Jeanette Smith and Leslie Hartman with Sauder Village; Pacific Asia Museum; Barbara Steinfeld with Travel Portland; the Cultural & Heritage Tourism Alliance; Cheryl Hargrove at Hargrove International; Partners in Tourism; Thomas Aageson with the Global Center for Cultural Entrepreneurship; Scott Gerloff with Heritage Travel/Goziac; and Amy Jordan Webb with the National Trust for Historic Preservation.

A very special thanks for helping to shape this book from concept to publication to Sheila Armstrong with the U.S. Cultural & Heritage Tourism

Marketing Council, and Beverly Barsook, Stephanie Peters and Kathy Cisar with the Museum Store Association. I would also like to thank Catherine Newton for her editing skills and Barbara Bricker with Small Miracles for book design.

Any errors or omissions are mine alone and I accept full responsibility. Your case studies and topics for future editions of "Marketing Cultural & Heritage Tourism" are welcome. Please e-mail ShopAmericaTours@aol.com.

Photography by Anne/Hilton Head Island Chamber of Commerce

Appendix A:
Glossary of Tourism Terms and Resources

Tourism communications are laced with a variety of terms and acronyms forming an entire language if their own. Everyone in the tourism industry will recall that this was a confusing area when starting out. To assist you, we've compiled many commonly used tourism terms, organizations and acronyms.

Tourism Terminology

Baby Boomers (Boomers): A generation defined as those born between 1946 and 1964.

Bed & Breakfast (B&B): Overnight accommodations, usually in a private home or boarding house, with a full American-style breakfast included in the rate.

Blocked Space: Reservations (for airline tickets, hotel accommodations, tours, etc.) made with suppliers by wholesalers or travel agents in anticipation of resale.

Booking/Reservation Form: Signed by customers purchasing tours, stating exactly which tour is being purchased. The form also outlines all liability.

Charter Flight: A flight booked exclusively for the use of a specific group or groups that are traveling on an inclusive tour charter program.

Commission: The amount of net income that travel agents or tour operators receive from a supplier for selling transportation, accommodations or other services.

Commissionable Rates: Includes a fee or commission that the travel agent or tour operator retains for sales of accommodations, transportation or services.

Confidential Tariff: A schedule of wholesale rates distributed in confidence to travel wholesalers and travel agents.

Consolidator: A person or company that forms groups to travel on air charters or at group fares on scheduled flights to increase sales, earn override commissions or reduce the possibility of tour cancellations.

Convention (Conference) & Visitors Bureau (CVB): Local tourism authority; also called the CVA, convention and visitors association or convention and visitors authority. Supported by membership fees and/or local taxes (often hotel taxes) with a mission to market all the visitor assets of a city or area.

Cultural and Heritage Tourism: Traveling to experience the places, artifacts and activities that authentically represent the stories and people of the past and present. It includes cultural, historic and natural resources.

***The Cultural Traveler* Guide:** Annual publication produced by the U.S. Cultural & Heritage Tourism Marketing Council and Shop America Alliance in partnership with the Museum Store Association to promote cultural and heritage travel to and within the United States.

Destination: The place to which a traveler is going, or any city, area, region or country being marketed as a single entity to tourists.

Destination Marketing Organization (DMO): The officially sanctioned convention and visitors bureau (CVB) or state tourism office.

Destination Management Company (DMC): Independent local firms that provide specialized visitor services and events for conventions or groups.

Double Occupancy Rate: The price per person for a room shared with another person.

Escort: A person, usually employed by a tour operator, who accompanies a tour from departure to return as guide or trouble-shooter; or a person who performs such functions only at the destination. The terms host-escort or host are often used, and are preferred, to describe this service.

Escorted Tour: A pre-arranged travel program, usually for a group, with escort service. Fully escorted tours may also use local guide services.

Familiarization Tour: Also called FAM tours. A complimentary or reduced-rate travel program for travel agents, airline or rail employees, or other travel buyers, designed to acquaint participants with specific destinations or suppliers and to stimulate the sale of travel. Familiarization tours are sometimes offered to travel journalists as research trips for the purpose of cultivating media coverage of specific travel products.

Fly/Drive: A traveler who purchases air and rental car packages only.

Foreign Independent Travel or Foreign Individual Travel (FIT): An international, pre-paid, unescorted tour that includes several travel elements such as accommodations, rental cars and sightseeing. A FIT operator specializes in preparing FIT documents at the request of retail travel agents. FITs usually receive travel vouchers to present to on-site services as verification of pre-payment.

Generation X (Gen X): A generation defined as those born between 1965 and 1983.

Generation Y (Gen Y): A generation defined as those born between 1984 and 2002.

Geotourism: Tourism that sustains or enhances the geographical character of the place being visited, including its environment, culture, aesthetics, heritage and the well-being of its residents.

Ground Operator: A company that provides local travel services, including transportation or guide services.

Group Leader: Escort of a group tour.

Group Tour: Twelve to 50 travelers together, usually on a motorcoach.

Historic District: A defined geographical area, which may be as small as a few contiguous buildings or as large as an entire neighborhood, central business district or community, within which historic properties associated with a particular time or theme in a community's history predominate. Often the collective significance of the district may be greater than that of any one building or archaeological site. As a planning tool, a historic district designation is often used to ensure the preservation of historic properties within the defined boundary, or to encourage reinvestment of the buildings.

Historic Property: A site that has qualities that make it significant in history, architecture, archaeology, engineering or culture; sometimes more specifically a site that is eligible for, or listed on, the National Register of Historic Places, or on a local or state register of significant sites.

Historic Resource: A historic building, site, structure, object or district that has the potential to benefit the community economically, educationally or in some other way if it is preserved.

Hostel: Inexpensive, supervised lodging; particularly used by young people or elders.

Hotel Package: A package offered by a hotel, sometimes consisting of no more than a room and breakfast; sometimes, especially at resort hotels, consisting of ground transportation, room, meals, attractions, shopping and other components.

Incentive Tour: A trip offered as a prize, usually by a company to stimulate employee sales or productivity, e.g., a golf package offered to top sales producers.

Incentives: Payment that tour operators expect for bringing you business, e.g., commissions, fees or gifts.

Itinerary: Travel schedule provided by a travel agent for the guest. A proposed or preliminary itinerary can be specific or rather vague. A final itinerary, however, provides all details—flight numbers, departure times, reservation confirmation numbers, etc.—and describes planned activities.

Landmark: A building, structure or object that marks the land—the familiar old building or other property—that provides orientation to a community or region.

Lure Brochure: 4" x 9" color brochure used in tourism marketing; rack-size format.

Meet & Greet: Attraction staff or ambassador meets the group tour when they arrive and provides information and at times small gifts.

Meeting Planners: Key contacts that plan conventions and corporate groups.

Motorcoach: Preferred name for a tour bus.

Museum: Institution devoted to the procurement, care, study and display of objects of lasting value or interest.

National Heritage Area: A place designated by the U.S. Congress, where natural, cultural, historic and recreational resources combine to form a cohesive, nationally distinctive landscape arising from patterns of human activity shaped by geography.

National Register of Historic Places: The nation's official roster of properties that should be preserved because of their significance in American history, architecture, archaeology, engineering or culture. The National Register recognizes important historic buildings, sites, structures, objects and districts. It includes properties of local, state or national importance.

Net Rate: Price of goods to be marked up for eventual resale to the consumer.

Online Travel Agent (OTA): Expedia, Travelocity, Orbitz, Priceline and many more that sell travel products (air, hotels, rental cars and more) directly to the consumer primarily via the Internet. They currently account for the majority of all travel sales in the United States.

Package Tour: A saleable travel product offering an inclusive price with several travel elements that would otherwise be purchased separately. Usually has a predetermined price, length of time and features, but can also offer options for separate purchase.

Packager: Anyone organizing a tour including pre-paid transportation and travel services, usually to more than one destination.

Person-Trip: The research term for one person taking one trip of 100 or more miles, one-way, away from home.

Preservation Commission: A governmental body appropriated by the mayor or city council under local law in some communities to advise on matters affecting historic resources; recommend official designation of significant historic properties and historic districts as local landmarks; and review proposed work to the community's officially designated local landmarks and in its official historic districts. Although the responsibilities and composition of commissions vary by local law, most have five to 10 members representing a variety of interests and areas of expertise related to the preservation and revitalization of historic properties.

Preservation Plan: A document that evaluates a community's historic resources and makes recommendations on steps that may be taken to ensure they are preserved and reused to the community's economic and social benefit.

Rack Rate: The official cost posted by a hotel, attraction or rental car agency, but not used by tour operators because they have discounted rates.

Receptive Operator: An international tour operator or travel agent based in the United States, specializing in services for incoming visitors, such as meeting them at the airport and facilitating their transfer to lodging facilities. Often sells and arranges cultural and heritage tours.

Rep: Representative for attractions in various markets.

RES Agent Training: Organized visits to offices of reservation agents by tour operators to train them on specific tourism products.

Retail Agency: Travel company selling directly to the public, sometimes a division of a wholesale and/or retail travel organization.

Sales Mission: Organized visit to offices of tour operators and wholesalers by small groups of suppliers; usually visiting several operators in a day in a series of meetings.

Silent/GI Generation: A generation defined as those born between 1927 and 1945.

Single Supplement: An extra charge assessed to individuals traveling alone who do not want to share accommodations.

Supplier: The actual producer of a unit of travel merchandise, such as a carrier, hotel or sightseeing operator.

Technical Visit: Tour designed for a special interest group, usually to visit a place of business with a common interest. The tour usually includes part business/part leisure and is customized for the group. Also called Technical Tours, which are popular with the Japanese market.

Tour: Any pre-arranged (but not necessarily pre-paid) journey to one or more places and back to the point of origin.

Tour Leader: A person with special qualifications to conduct a particular travel group, such as a botanist who conducts a garden tour.

Tour Operator: A company that plans, creates and/or markets inclusive tours and/or performs tour services for travel agents and consumers.

Tour Wholesaler: Same as tour operator, but with activities limited to selling product to travel agents only.

Tourism: The business of providing and marketing services and facilities for pleasure travelers. Thus, the concept of tourism is of direct concern to governments and carriers and the lodging, restaurant and entertainment industries, and of indirect concern to virtually every industry and business in the world.

Travel Agent: The individual who sells travel services and packaged tours, issues tickets and provides other travel services to the traveler at the retail level.

Travel Aggregator: Travel marketer that organizes/aggregates a large group of travel options or experiences under one umbrella sales program.

Examples include CityPASS, Smart Destination's Go City Cards and Shop America Tours.

Travel Reseller: Travel agents and tour operators that sell travel experiences owned by others; hence, they are called travel resellers.

Travel Trade Media: Publications that reach tour operators and travel agents with travel news and views.

TripAdvisor.com: Top travel social media site where travelers review and rate their experiences.

Vouchers: Documents issued by a tour operator to be exchanged for accommodations, meals, sightseeing, admission tickets, etc., or redeemable for discounts, coupon book or other incentives at the attraction.

Wholesaler: A company that usually creates and markets inclusive tours and FITs for sale through travel agents. Typically sells nothing at retail, but also does not always create its own product; also less likely to perform local services.

Organizations

Advisory Council on Historic Preservation (ACHP): Works to promote the preservation, enhancement, and productive use of America's historic resources; advises the U.S. President and U.S. Congress on national historic preservation policy. *www.achp.gov*

Alliance of National Heritage Areas: Informal organization of federally-designated heritage areas and corridors, committed to raising awareness of the benefits of national heritage areas to the public; fosters educational opportunities and partnerships among organizations in the heritage development field. *www.nationalheritageareas.com*

American Association of Museums (AAM): National organization representing every type of museum (art, history, science, military and maritime, and youth museums, as well as aquariums, zoos, botanical gardens, arboretums, historic sites, and science and technology centers), addressing its members' needs and enhancing the ability of museums to serve the public interest. *www.aam-us.org*

American Association for State and Local History (AASLH): Nonprofit organization providing leadership, service and support for its members who preserve and interpret state and local history in order to make the past more meaningful in American society. *www.aaslh.org*

American Automobile Association (AAA): Organization providing its members with travel, insurance, financial and automotive-related services. Also operates retail travel agencies. *www.aaa.com*

American Bus Association (ABA): Trade association representing charter and intercity bus companies, as well as motorcoach owners and operators focused on group tours for international and domestic, seniors and student group markets. *www.buses.org*

American Craft Council: National, nonprofit educational organization dedicated to promoting the understanding and appreciation of contemporary American craft. *www.craftcouncil.org*

American Hotel & Lodging Association (AH&LA): Trade association for the lodging industry; provides its members with tools and resources to achieve bottom-line savings and ensure a positive business climate for the lodging industry. *www.ahma.com*

American Society of Travel Agents (ASTA): Trade association of retail travel agents; facilitates the business of selling travel through effective representation, shared knowledge and the enhancement of professionalism. *www.asta.org*

Americans for the Arts: National organization that strives to make arts more accessible to every adult and child in America by working with cultural organizations, arts and business leaders and individuals to foster leadership, education and information that will encourage support for the arts and culture in U.S. communities. *www.artsusa.org*

Association of Retail Travel Agents (ARTA): Trade association of North American travel agents. *www.arta.travel*

Corporation for Travel Promotion (CTP): Public/private partnership with the mission of promoting increased international travel to the United States. *www.corporationfortravelpromotion.com*

Cultural & Heritage Tourism Alliance (CHTA): Informal group of U.S. practitioners responsible for cultural and heritage tourism programs in states, cities and regions, promoting the integration of culture and heritage into a broad range of economic development strategies. *www.chtalliance.com*

Destination Marketing Association International (DMAI): Formerly the International Association of Convention & Visitors Bureaus (IACVB), this worldwide association is dedicated to improving the effectiveness of destination marketing organizations. *www.destinationmarketing.org*

Destination & Travel Foundation: Formerly the DMAI Foundation, a nonprofit research and charitable foundation that combines the resources of the DMAI and the U.S. Travel Association to focus on providing innovative solutions to travel challenges and ongoing education on travel and tourism. *www.destinationmarketing.org*

Discover America Partnership: An effort led by some of America's foremost business leaders to strengthen America's image around the globe. It aims to empower the American people as the nation's ambassadors by increasing their opportunities to interact with international visitors. *www.poweroftravel.org*

Institute of Museum and Library Services (IMLS): An independent federal agency that fosters leadership, innovation and a lifetime of learning by creating strong libraries and museums that connect people to information and ideas. *www.imls.gov*

International Association of Amusement Parks & Attractions (IAAPA): The trade association of amusement parks, water parks, family entertainment centers, zoos, aquariums, attractions and museums, and the manufacturers and suppliers that serve them. *www.iaapa.org*

The Luxury Marketing Council: Monitors trends and facilitates partnerships to market to the nearly nine million luxury travelers (those with incomes of $1 million or more) in the United States. *www.luxurycouncil.com*

Museum Store Association (MSA): International organization representing museum store professionals worldwide from more than 1,600 institutions. By encouraging high standards of professional competence and conduct, MSA helps museum store managers better serve their institutions and the public. *www.MuseumStoreAssociation.org*

National Assembly of State Arts Agencies (NASAA): Membership organization of the nation's state and jurisdictional arts agencies that advances and promotes a meaningful role for the arts in the lives of individuals, families and communities throughout the United States. *www.nasaa-arts.org*

National Council of Attractions (NCA): Umbrella trade group within the U.S. Travel Association that serves as a forum for a broad group of attractions from amusement parks and historic homes to zoos and aquariums. *www.ustravel.org/member-services/national-council-of-attractions*

National Endowment for the Arts (NEA): Independent agency of the federal government serving the public good by nurturing human creativity, supporting community spirit and fostering appreciation of the excellence and diversity of America's artistic accomplishments through grant-making, leadership initiatives, partnerships and public information. *www.arts.endow.gov*

National Endowment for the Humanities (NEH): Independent grant-making agency of the U.S. government dedicated to supporting research, education, preservation and public programs in the humanities. *www.neh.gov*

National Park Service (NPS): A division of the U.S. Department of the Interior, NPS preserves unimpaired the natural and cultural resources and values of the national park system for the enjoyment, education and inspiration of this and future generations. It also oversees the National Register of Historic Places and assists federally-designated national heritage areas. *www.nps.gov*

National Register of Historic Places: Administered by the National Park Service (NPS), the register is part of a national program to coordinate and support public and private efforts to identify, evaluate and protect the historic and archeological resources of the United States. *www.cr.nps.gov/nr*

National Tour Association (NTA): Trade association of tourism professionals, including motorcoach tour operators, attractions and group travel buyers, involved in the growth and development of the packaged travel industry. *www.ntaonline.com*

National Trust for Historic Preservation: National nonprofit organization dedicated to saving historic places and revitalizing America's communities by providing advice and assistance. It also manages the nation's first cultural heritage tourism program and the National Trust Main Street Center, a program that pioneered the "main street" approach to commercial district revitalization. *www.preservationnation.org*

Office of Travel & Tourism Industries (OTTI): The federal agency responsible for tracking and analyzing international visitation to the United States. Its role is to expand travel and tourism business opportunities for employment and economic growth. Works with the U.S. Secretary of Commerce to organize the Travel & Tourism Advisory Board (TTAB) to provide direction for US tourism policy. *www.tinet.ita.doc.gov*

Partners in Tourism: Coalition among national associations and federal agencies broadly representing the arts, humanities, heritage and tourism organizations around the country, dedicated to building a common agenda for cultural tourism. *www.culturalheritagetourism.org*

President's Committee on the Arts and the Humanities (PCAH): Helps to underscore the civic, social, educational and historical value of arts and humanities in the life of America. It recognizes cultural excellence, engages in research, initiates special projects and stimulates private funding. *www.pcah.gov*

Receptive Services Association of America (RSAA): Organization of receptive tour operators and suppliers. Its focus is on working with suppliers, regulatory agencies and travel promotion bureaus to improve the quality of travel-related services for foreign visitors. *www.rsana.com*

Shop America Alliance LLC (SAA): Premier shopping/tourism organization representing more than 200 of America's top shopping centers, outlets, retailers and destinations (including museum stores). Develops and markets packaged shopping, dining and cultural tours. *www.ShopAmericaTours.com*

Society of American Travel Writers (SATW): An association of journalists, photographers and media relations professionals whose primary occupation is reporting about travel destinations. *www.satw.org*

State Offices of Tourism: Most states have an official office of tourism funded by state tax dollars and/or public/private partnerships with a mission of promoting the state's tourism assets for economic development.

Travel and Tourism Research Association (TTRA): A professional society of market researchers specializing in the travel industry; it facilitates access to numerous sources of information to support research efforts. *www.ttra.com*

U.S. Cultural & Heritage Tourism Marketing Council: An independent, for-profit organization of destination marketing organizations and marketing professionals dedicated to developing cultural and heritage tourism packages that offer unique and innovative cultural and heritage experiences to visitors to and within the United States. *www.uscht.com*

U.S. Travel Association: Formerly the Travel Industry Association (TIA), the nonprofit trade organization of companies and government agencies representing all segments of the travel industry formed to promote and facilitate travel to and within the United States. *www.USTravel.org*

Visit USA Committees: International, membership-based organizations that provide in-country marketing services in selected parts of the world. *www.ustravel.org/marketing/international-programs/visit-usa-committees*

World Travel & Tourism Council (WTTC): Forum for business leaders in the travel and tourism industry. With chief executives of some 100 of the world's leading travel and tourism companies as its members, WTTC has a unique mandate and overview on all matters related to travel and tourism. WTTC works to raise awareness of travel and tourism as one of the world's largest industries, supporting more than 258 million jobs and generating 9.1 percent of world grow domestic product (GDP). *www.wttc.org*

Annual Tourism Tradeshows

Active America Travel Summit: Destination development conference for the Japanese and Chinese inbound tourism market that brings together top tour operators with invited suppliers and destinations to develop new tour opportunities. *www.activeamerica.net*

American Bus Marketplace: Produced by the American Bus Association (ABA), this annual appointment show allows bus owners and tour operators to meet with travel industry representatives from destination marketing organizations. *www.buses.org*

Brazilian Travel Agencies Association (ABAV): Offers the top international Brazilian travel tradeshow; held in a different Brazilian city each year. *www.abav.com.br*

DMAI Conference: Presented by Destination Marketing Association International each summer for DMAI members/DMOs. *www.destinationmarketing.org*

eTourism Summit: A travel industry conference and marketplace that focuses on e-commerce and marketing international tourism. *www.etourismsummit.com*

Expo Vacaciones: Top Mexican travel tradeshow that promotes tourism to the United States; held annually in Mexico City. *www.expovacaciones.eu*

Go West Summit: Premier business-oriented, international annual travel tradeshow selling the American West (Arizona, California, Colorado, Idaho, Montana, Nevada, New Mexico, Oregon, Utah, Washington and Wyoming). *www.gowestsummit.com*

International Pow Wow: The largest international travel trade event held each year in the United States with more than 5,000 participants; organized by U.S. Travel Association. *www.powwowonline.com*

ITB Berlin: World's largest travel trade event with more than 65,000 delegates; held each March in Berlin, Germany. *www.itb-berlin.com*

La Cumbre: Largest Latin American travel trade event in the United States; held each fall. *www.lacumbre.com*

Marketing Outlook Forum: Organized by the U.S. Travel Association, an annual meeting and tourism research/ idea exchange held each fall. *www.ustravel.org*

Meeting Professionals International (MPI): Holds an annual conference for meeting planners and travel suppliers. *www.mpiweb.org*

National Tour Association (NTA): Holds an annual convention and spring meeting for its membership of national tourism professionals each year, focusing on group tours to and within North America. *www.ntaonline.com*

ONE Travel Conference for Shopping, Dining & Cultural Tourism: Annual sales meeting and educational forum for shopping, dining and cultural tourism produced each January by Shop America Alliance and the U.S. Cultural & Heritage Tourism Marketing Council. *www.OneTravelConference.com*

Receptive Services Association of America (RSAA Summit): Holds an annual summit for receptive tour operators and suppliers; alternates each year between New York and Florida. *www.rsana.com*

World Travel Market (WTM): Major travel tradeshow held in London each year in November. Provides an opportunity for the global travel trade industry to meet, network, negotiate, conduct business and stay abreast of trends. *www.wtmlondon.com*

Common Acronyms

AAM: American Association of Museums

B&B: Bed and Breakfast

CHT: Cultural Heritage Travel

CTP: Corporation for Travel Promotion

CVA: Convention & Visitors Association

CVB: Convention (Conference) & Visitors Bureau

DMO: Destination Marketing Organization

DOC: Department of Commerce

FAM: Familiarization Tour

FIT: Foreign Independent Traveler or Frequent Independent Traveler

GSA: General Sales Agent

MSA: Museum Store Association

OTA: Online Travel Agent

OTTI: Office of Travel & Tourism Industries (division of U.S. Department of Commerce)

SAA: Shop America Alliance

TTAB: Travel & Tourism Advisory Board (overseen by U.S. Department of Commerce)

USCHT: U.S. Cultural & Heritage Tourism Marketing Council

USDOC: U.S. Department of Commerce

Appendix B:
For More Information

About the Museum Store Association (MSA)

Founded in 1955, the Museum Store Association is a nonprofit, international association organized to advance the success of cultural commerce and of the professionals engaged in it. By encouraging high standards of professional competence and conduct, MSA helps retail professionals at cultural institutions better serve their organizations and the public. MSA also is focused on helping increase awareness about museum stores as unique shopping destinations for tourists and cultural travelers.

Governed by a seven-member board of directors, the Association serves approximately 1,650 institutional members and nearly 725 exhibitor affiliates. A staff of nine full-time employees operates from MSA's headquarters in Denver, Colo. For more information, go to www.MuseumStoreAssociation.org.

About Shop America Alliance (SAA)

Founded in 1998, Shop America Alliance LLC is a travel trade association with a mission to promote shopping and dining tourism experiences. Representing hundreds of shopping and dining tourism destinations in North America, SAA co-produces the annual ONE Travel Conference on Shopping, Dining and Cultural Tourism and the SASI-ONE Awards. SAA publishes *Shop America Magazine*, co-publishes *The Cultural Traveler* guide and markets more than 200 shopping, dining and cultural tours in 40 cities at www.shopamericatours.com, www.theculturaltraveler.com and through leading tour operators and travel partners. For more information visit www.shopamericatours.com, www.ONEtravelconference.com, or contact Rosemary McCormick at shopamericatours@aol.com or (707) 224-3795.

About the U.S. Cultural & Heritage Tourism Marketing Council (USCHT)

The U.S. Cultural and Heritage Tourism Marketing Council LLC is a travel trade association with a mission to market U.S. cultural and heritage tourism experiences both nationally and internationally. Co-founded in 2007 by Sheila Armstrong who serves as executive director and Rosemary McCormick, president of Shop America Alliance LLC, USCHT represents leading U.S. tourism destinations, attractions and travel partners engaged in marketing U.S. cultural and heritage to travelers throughout the United States and around the world. The organization co-publishes *The Cultural Traveler* guide and markets leading cultural and heritage experiences at www.TheCulturalTraveler.com.

The U.S. Cultural & Heritage Tourism Marketing Council membership is open to all U.S. cultural and heritage organizations and destinations engaged in cultural and heritage travel. For more information about the USCHT and the benefits of membership, visit www.uscht.com or contact Sheila Armstrong at uschtmarketing@aol.com or (843) 341-6392.

The Cultural & Heritage Traveler Study

The 131-page PDF version of The Cultural & Heritage Traveler Study is available for purchase from Mandala Research for $350 or at a discount rate of $175 for members of the Museum Store Association, American Association of Museums and the U.S. Cultural & Heritage Tourism Marketing Council. To order, contact Laura Mandala at Laura@MandalaResearch.com or (703) 820-1041.

Speaker's Bureau Opportunity

An expert presenter from the U.S. Cultural & Heritage Tourism Marketing Council, or one of its partners, is available to present a PowerPoint on "Marketing Cultural & Heritage Tourism" at meetings and conferences with 25 or more attendees. The only cost is reimbursement of the speaker's approved travel expenses. For more information, contact Sheila Armstrong at uschtmarketing@aol.com or (843) 341-6392.

First published 2011 by Museum Store Association

Published 2016 by Routledge
2 Park Square, Milton Park, Abingdon, Oxon OX14 4RN
711 Third Avenue, New York, NY 10017, USA

Routledge is an imprint of the Taylor & Francis Group, an informa business

Copyright

ISBN 13: 978-1-61132-877-6 (pbk)

Chef Poon, Philadelphia